The CREEP Among Us * Anne Penn

The

# CREEP

## Among Us

Alleged Serial Killer

Golden State Killer

Original Night Stalker

East Area Rapist

Visalia Ransacker

Joseph James DeAngelo

By

Anne Penn AKA Laurie

The CREEP Among Us * Anne Penn

The CREEP Among Us * Anne Penn

Copyright 2018    By ANNE PENN. All rights reserved

No part of this book may be reproduced, stored in a retrieval system, or transmitted in any form or by any means without the written permission of the author.

Printed in the United States of America

Cover Graphics and customization of design created by Tim

Because of the dynamic nature of the Internet any Web addresses or links contained in this book may have changed since publication and may no longer be valid.

Disclaimer: The information in this book is true as best as I can discover as of October 2018. Although there was a 100% DNA match linking Joseph James DeAngelo to the crimes of the East Area Rapist, Original Night Stalker, Golden State Killer **we do have to keep in mind and believe that a person in the United States of America is innocent until proven guilty in a court of law.** We have to have a presumption of innocence until he has been tried and been found guilty or he is acquitted in a court of law. That being said I must tell the story and the facts that are known about the logistics of this particular man as known to this point. I do so in order to try and make sense of the details for myself. I am a very curious person who needs to know as much information as possible to resolve the story and to begin to at last try to let it go. Mr. DeAngelo may never be tried, he could confess, he could pass away before the truth becomes known. We shall see how the story ends. This publication is part of what I needed to know, how I felt in the journey and what I thought. It is also about facts pertaining to the geography, the logistics, placing Mr. DeAngelo in the areas these crimes occurred so long ago. Thank you for your understanding. My intention is to do no harm ultimately.

**This book is dedicated to my mother Anita who shared her love of books with me early on, who made sure I learned to play the violin and who became my cheering section especially in the last few years. She passed away October 6, 2018. Thanks Mom.**

## CRIMINAL MINDS

## OBSESSION

**"Obsession is not necessarily a path traveled**

**Only by serial killers**

**Mission oriented, driven by need based desires,**

**Profilers and serial killers**

**Overlap in more ways than**

**One would imagine"**

Prologue

And now a new journey begins. After 42 years a suspect is in custody at the Sacramento County Jail, not far from where his attacks began in 1976. A man who has a face, and a name at last sits there locked behind bars. I do not want to call him by name. He does not deserve one. Not really. He was masquerading all of these years as a person, a human. A man with a life such as we may discover it was. He hid in plain sight with children now grown, and a family life. Well at least it was meant to look like a family life. Disclosures say that the DeAngelo's had been separated for the last 27 years, but not divorced.

What will we discover over time? We know what he did. At least we can name 13 of his murder victims. Are there more? I would think so. There were at least 50 rapes as well. As Law Enforcement connects the dots the old fashioned way, gathering evidence not only that this man was in each area when the murders happened, they look for other unsolved murders that may be connected to this serial killer.

This man now referred to as JJD on the proboards and other places via internet discussions is currently not taking responsibility and has not been talking to Law Enforcement so far. At least that is what is known through the grapevine. Law Enforcement is very tight lipped as they investigate this man's whereabouts for the last 42 years. They have to be in order to present a case at trial.

Many will write about the crimes of this serial killer. There will be much hearsay and rumor. When all is said and done this man may not live long enough to stand trial. The wheels of justice by rights should move quickly in this case. Because of the many jurisdictions involved in this case it will be complicated. At least as I write this book the decision appears to be made that the trial will move forward in Sacramento. The jurisdictions will all try him in Sacramento. To me it seems the way it should be because of all the victims in that place.

How can one not truly think they have the right man when his DNA is a 100% match to the perp who left his fluids behind those many years ago? Now the perpetrator is 72 years old. If it takes five years to go to trial, he will be an old man. We shall see how this story plays out. All of us have been watching from the beginning. Us meaning those of us who have known of the creeps' existence since 1976 and possibly before.

The quote I have used in my previous books about fear is what has turned out to fit this serial killer perfectly. This man, this one who now justly sits in a box while we wait to see how many other lives were stolen by him, how many other crimes can be proven without doubt. This man used his power and what he knew to protect us in order to harm us. He did hold our fear in his hands and he ultimately did show that fear to all of us. He held that for 42 years. He did see what power there was in manipulating us, in scaring us. This elusive man now has a face and a name, but to me his name is CREEP.

The CREEP Among Us * Anne Penn

## Table of Contents

Prologue

Introduction

Monikers

Chapter One  The Crimes Known VR

Chapter Two  More Crimes

Chapter Three  Auburn

Chapter Four Crimes in East Sacramento & South Sacramento

Chapter Five  Possible Connections to other crimes

Chapter Six Why was he not caught in the beginning?

Chapter Seven  Murder Victims

Chapter Eight Lack Of Cooperation

Chapter Nine Larry Crompton

Written by Larry Crompton

Chapter Ten Mark Smith A Question of Ballistics

Chapter Eleven What made him so evil?

Chapter Twelve What we know about JJD so far

Crimes After 1980 possibles and Sue's Story

Chapter Thirteen DNA Geneaology connected

Chapter Fourteen  Who Am I? Why Do I Care?

The CREEP Among Us * Anne Penn

Side Notes, Thank You's, Violent Crimes, Bibliography

Page Numbers

| Chapter One | Page 26 |
| Chapter Two | Page 57 |
| Chapter Three | Page 64 |
| Chapter Four | Page 104 |
| Chapter Five | Page 123 |
| Chapter Six | Page 158 |
| Chapter Seven | Page 184 |
| Chapter Eight | Page 199 |
| Chapter Nine | Page 221 |
| Chapter Ten | Page 229 |
| Chapter Eleven | Page 237 |
| Chapter Twelve | Page 242 |
| Chapter Thirteen | Page 264 |
| Chapter Fourteen | Page 273 |

Endings Side Notes, Thank You's

Bibliography          Page 292

## Introduction

Here is the thing……….

This is not a story told with beautiful prose or fantastic words where one has to stop to look up the meaning – it is not a tale – a fairytale that one can walk away from feeling lovely.

Sometimes stories that are real, raw stories can be told as in a conversation with real words and feelings, sometimes repeated as if to reconcile the story, to try to digest or comprehend things that are incomprehensible

This story is about something so brutal, so horrific one can find no words in the end, only silence that falls as we wait for answers. This story is about a man who went off the rails, one who used what he knew to protect us, in order to harm us. Not individually, but as a whole. He set out to make individual victims pay, and all of us as a society, our communities. He knew how to inflict pain and suffering on all of us.

I took this on to exorcise the beast, to shed light on the box carefully sealed in the darkest corners of my mind, to dust it off long ago covered, lid tightly sealed because what was in it, put there almost forty years ago was just too dark, too scary to touch.

Inside waited the details of murders of people loved by someone I loved as a father and friend, someone who meant a lot to me. Their loss was everyone's loss. All of the murders were all of our losses.

I do not know how one can ever get the visual of a crime so real, so brutal out of one's mind. Broken are we who hear it, never repaired, never the same. Eventually the images are shown on the internet for all to see. Less scary in some way from what lived in my mind. Broken and bloody fireplace log, pieces splintered, blood spatter, bed linens pulled up over bodies in their own home, in their own bedroom where they are supposed to be safe.

Some creep – stalking, watching, arrogant enough to get right up close. Peering in windows, hiding under bushes. Childish behaviors calling on the phone, terrorizing, breathing, whispering "I'm gonna kill you." Leaving after raping and bludgeoning if all goes as planned.

Soft, long hair bloody, not moving taking a last breath, never to laugh or sing again at the beauty of a day.

Studying the mindset of a serial killer soon after the murders. Trying to understand and somehow look at this in a clinical, logical way. Detach, desensitize, except for the FEAR – fear at how insecure one can truly be in our own home. Sticks in sliding glass doors, shades drawn at dusk. Worry at windows where one can see in, but one cannot see out. Who is watching? Who will see you and then decide…. Doors locked and checked again.

This book (Murder On His Mind) was designed to try and help find a killer of the most AWFUL kind, one who raises the spine in fear – determination to get the word out. Who do you know? Did you know him? Think back, this is how it was back then. How did we miss him? This book designed to heal my mind even if this monster is never caught.

Stay the fear, quiet the fight or flight response. This is the story of a rapist and murderer who shattered a time, a place, and people. Lots of people. The reality for many has been the gut wrenching horror and brutality to wrestle with every day since the very beginning of these crimes.

Me telling my son when he was small that police were here to protect us. Many, but not all. How did I, how did we walk on the same streets as a man like this? One who hated so much.?

I could not ever get the images out of my mind, a man watching in the dark, watching private moments between a man and woman. Stalking, coming in looking around knowing he would be back. To take EVERYTHING from them. Everything, every drop of humanity, everything decent and good. All that is left is evil and hate until he exits taking everything once good. Leaving the shatteredness, the splinters, the drops of evidence, the silence. The sound had been loud enough to fill the room, your senses, the ugly brutal sound. Stillness left behind, two or three days, bodies found, the story told over and over into infinity. It's over now. At least for some.

    I wrote this when I was feeling extremely frustrated over the cases even after for all intents and purposes as we wait for the slow wheels of justice to turn JJD will never walk free again. We will hear bits and pieces for years to come confirming all of the awful truths about this man. The reality of this even though the monster now sits in a cage is we now have to discover how we feel about this individually and collectively.

I slowly read the redacted pages of the arrest warrant just released a bit at a time because what is in the warrant for JJD's arrest has been known to those of us who have followed, investigated and read about these crimes. All the documents tell us is that JJD is believed to be the terrible man who prowled outside houses, broke in through windows and doors, never caring who he hurt, and simply wanting to wreak havoc anywhere he went. What a cruel subhuman individual.

For those of you that had never heard of these cases or these stories until recently I feel compelled to say that you are lucky to not have known sooner. All of the victims of this man had their lives changed forever. The effect of the attacks 32 years up until 42 years ago and beyond means that all of the victims of this man have had to live with what he did to them for so many decades. We have been there since the beginning, from Visalia to Sacramento and all of the other jurisdictions in which he raped, prowled, stalked, attacked and gave each and every one of the people who were aware of his existence a feeling of unrest. Our calm as communities was never the same. We have lived with these stories, the post-traumatic stress involved for close enough to a half a century. By the time this criminal is brought to trial or a deal is made or he just dies in jail we will not be finished with the story. I envy those who sit on the fringes and who are fascinated by true crime. If true crime has never touched you or your family, I wish you well; and I pray it never comes to visit you. There are so many victims of violent crimes out there living with murder of a loved one, the loss of innocence about how safe we all really are not. Eventually because this man was not caught in his beginnings he had the opportunity to evolve or morph into the absolute worst version of himself he could be. As he sits in jail you can see the evil beneath the surface. I personally believe in the criminal justice system when it comes to the ideal that a man or woman is supposed to be innocent until proven guilty, but how can one say that in this case?

The system must change to keep up with the technology of today. There are times when DNA can be wrong. For example, a criminalist can transfer his or her own DNA to a sample or have their DNA show up on evidence. If we only believed that the only way the DNA could show up on evidence is that the person is guilty or they had to have committed these crimes our criminal justice system would be compromised and limited to very narrow thinking. In the case of JJD and the sheer number of DNA sample matches to the man and to the crimes, science, rape kits, it would seem there is no other way the DNA could have come from each scene that connects JJD to the crimes unless he himself is actually the evil doer and the guilty party. He has to be the guilty party with his 100% DNA match. Yet, we will have to connect him geographically, timelines, physical evidence matched, eye witness testimony. All of the old ways of backing up the case, against JJD must be gathered. The prosecution must do this thing well and the right way in order to see that justice is served and that the victims and family members of these crimes finally see justice at last in their lifetimes. The defense has the right to review discovery evidence, get up to speed on all aspects of the case.

This case will take a long time to resolve even with a 100% DNA match. This case will set precedents, change laws and be complex until the end.

Back in the beginning when JJD came to town it was the decade of the sixties. Sacramento was a pretty quiet place that still felt the conversion of fields turned into asphalt. There were fields left all around. Cows still could be seen frequently as they had not given up the sleepy farms surrounding the area. I used to love going for drives out off Gerber Road where eventually I learned to drive a stick shift. You could still see then that not long ago, in Sacramento's past there had been a gold rush in the foothills all around the area. In the 1800's in downtown Sacramento Sutter's Fort was built not far now from the Sacramento County Jail.

JJD went to High School in Folsom, CA. Not far from Sacramento yet it truly was still a rural place complete with the old town feel and beautiful churches. Even now all these years later these old towns still exist to remind of what once was during the Gold Rush. These places all around Sacramento had been where I would go as a sixteen-year-old just turned loose with my driver's license and an old Volkswagen. I drove so much through Sutter Creek, Georgetown and Downieville in the foothills, and then on other days heading my bug out to the roads that ventured to Jackson and Ione, lots of little hills and dips in the road that one could drive fast and fly just for a moment. I would drive out on those country roads everywhere, to Lodi and Galt, Stockton. One day as I was speeding around those old roads my Volkswagen gave up the ghost. I had worn it out and blown the engine. Stuck out in Galt which seemed so far from home that day.

In the 1960's when Joe DeAngelo showed up in our town hailing from New York, the town he arrived in was young and innocent in all the best ways. The freeways had not been built. Conceived of yes, but I recall driving to Folsom Lake on the only road one could take. It was what we now only use as the old frontage road, but it was the road one would take from South Sacramento where I grew up to Folsom Lake. We would pass an Orange Julius on the left side of the street, and a drive up hamburger stand called Walk-Ups. The Thunderbird Drive-In still existed and was always busy in the summer. It was in Rancho Cordova not far from the small shopping center my dad would bring me to three summers in a row to find the busses all there waiting to pick up our girl scout troops. It was hot in the middle of summer. All the 10 to 13-year-old girls would board the busses. Waving out the back of the bus looking somewhat questioning because some of us had never been to camp before. I would spend the next two weeks with other girls from all over Sacramento. The busses would drive up on Highway 50 towards the mountains and to a dirt road not far from Pacific House. This is still a very small blip of a town right off the freeway. We would spend two weeks, camping, singing, hiking, and swimming in amongst the trees. We would take pictures of one another and promise after two weeks to stay in touch. We had become bonded and connected. Back then two weeks seemed forever. My new friends signed my girl scout autograph book. In 1966, 67 and 68 we were 10, 11 and 12.

At the end of the two weeks we would cry to leave one another. My dad would show up again in the parking lot in Rancho Cordova. Waiting for the busses to bring us back into the very hot summers of Sacramento, seeming hotter now after leaving the fresh, cool mountain air. My friends going back to their neighborhoods, in Carmichael, Citrus Heights, Fair Oaks, Orangevale, and Rancho Cordova. It seemed so far away from where I went to South Sacramento back then. My friends finished growing up in East Sacramento becoming young women in those neighborhoods. Young ladies now at 19 and 20 years old in 1976. In 1976 the East Area Rapist came to our awareness.

But, my friends were there in those attack areas. Was Ann who we nicknamed Banana at camp one of his victims? Every time I look at my old girl scout autograph book complete with pictures I wonder all these years later, who did he attack, terrorize and rape that I knew when we were children? Why should this have happened to them? Why should that thought have to creep into my mind along with my happy memories of times spent as an innocent child? Why did this man pick our town? To destroy our peace? Why should we, any of us have had to worry not only about the East Area Rapist who would consume most of Sacramento for two plus years

1976-1979 but, there were a few other rapists terrorizing Sacramento at the same time. Our innocence would have slowly changed over time as it did in every city in every state. It would have slowly given way to the awareness that evil could come to people, but it would have been a slower and less brutal an awakening.

In 1976 the East Area Rapist did come to our awareness. After several months of attacks where there was a media blackout about the crimes an article finally shows up in the Sacramento Bee and the Sacramento Union. During a neighborhood town hall meeting the discussion had turned to the attacks that had not been mentioned to the public by law enforcement or the media. We had been unaware for the most part, but the victims in the East part of town had been speaking to one another about what was going on. They had talked to each other in this small area of Sacramento County. At the town hall meeting they finally asked law enforcement what was going on? We had been unaware and so could not take steps to protect ourselves for 8 months.

How many women were attacked and raped by EAR and others? The rape laws were at this time frame in our history laughable if one could actually laugh about such things. The punishments handed out if one were ever prosecuted, laughable. But, that is for another chapter.

In the 1960's they began to build the freeway's forever connecting us as a town forgetting the frontage roads, watching as the concrete and steel pillars arrived standing with the steel rebar lines staring at the sky before the upper freeway became connected to them. Watching when it was all done taking the 99 freeway to 50 heading towards Rancho Cordova and Folsom Lake. Faster yes, but then there were the people driving this new freeway throwing trash out the window. Bags of trash hitting the median to rest there. Before the littering laws came into being, no doubt to try and keep these highways looking new and keeping debris out of our way so we could go fast, ever faster as we drove quickly from downtown to the hills passing East Sacramento and the American River on our way.

On the other side of town, the I-5 freeway also began to appear. The frontage roads taken there heading out from Downtown, to Sutterville Road and going to what we called and still do call the Pocket Area. Running parallel to the Sacramento River this new highway would be an alternate, new route to take us all to Southern California eventually. But, for now the I-5 only ran along on the South side not far from Freeport and still ended. It was not a complete highway yet when the East Area Rapist ran amok. Likely he still took the 99 freeway to get to Stockton, Modesto and Fresno. He knew like I did that it was faster, still more direct.

Last year in a phone conversation I had with Paul Holes we were talking about the travels of EAR and the fact that it seemed he was hopping off the freeway near Danville and Concord. Possibly driving south via Highway 80 – 680 and 580 dropping into areas, attacking and then vanishing once again. We talked about two of the attack areas in Sacramento before EAR left. I lived off Riverside and Seamas Avenue very near attack 32. I was discussing with Paul what you could see from Casilada and Riverside not far from the I-5 Freeway. The subject came up that one could see the overpass and we discussed how he may have entered the neighborhood on foot as we know he left on foot likely running up on the levee above the Sacramento River. He mentioned something about the I-5 freeway and I said Paul the I-5 freeway was not complete yet in 1978. It ran all the way from up north to down past Sutterville Road, not far from Seamas really and then stopped. I told Paul the freeway had not been completed until after EAR moved south. His reply to me was "I did not know that." I knew because I grew up there, lived there and knew if I wanted to get to Stockton my choices were to hop off the partially built I-5 freeway, take the frontage roads or hop over to Highway 99 to go all the way South which would take you to Fresno and Bakersfield and finally towards Los Angeles.

When one looks at the geography, topography and travel routes one cannot assume that all the connections had yet been made in all of the highways surrounding Sacramento. I-5 was built last. At one time in 1975, 76 I worked out in Freeport near AJ Bumps restaurant. One could only get there on the frontage roads out in the country that ran parallel to the Sacramento River which eventually leads down to the Delta and the San Joaquin Valley. In 1978 one still had to get off the I-5 and travel the frontage roads south until I-5 could be picked up again.

When I told Paul about the freeway ending in and around the pocket area back in 1978 his tone was one of surprise. He did not know about this fine detail because he had not lived there. Unless one researches every avenue and every detail not many knew that the I-5 freeway was not joined together and completed until 1979. These details matter when you try to trace the East Area Rapists travels considering exact routes, what he was thinking, how easy it would be to drop off the highway, attack and move on. We know that the East Area Rapist attacked in Sacramento and on occasion would cross over into other jurisdictions. One can safely assume and one is probably correct in thinking that when the East Area Rapist left to attack in Stockton, Fresno and other places not far from Sacramento that he took Highway 99. One can also assume that when the EAR moved South that his travels were on the Highway 80 freeway out of Sacramento moving onto 580 or 680 depending on where he was of a mind to attack. EAR also apparently had a place to stay down south eventually and even actually moved down South for a time with his wife and daughter.

In this book I will include maps of roads travelled and time frames required to get from one place to another. EAR came to California as a teen. He learned his way around during those times mostly on frontage roads and country roads around and through the areas. He was not travelling main roads as he grew and moved on from high school and college. He knew very intricately how to get from one place to another without travelling on the freeway mostly constructed then. He knew the rivers, the creeks and waterways intimately. He knew where the parks were in every neighborhood and the schools which were surrounded with middle class homes. He had studied all of the ways one could travel quickly and quietly in the dark. He knew he could ride a bike down pathways and in areas no car chasing him could follow. He knew to use different vehicles different stolen bikes never leaving a fingerprint or any real trail of evidence to link him to any of the attacks. He studied this as a teen, went to college majoring in Criminal Justice. The junior college he selected was in a rural area along one of those country roads at the time. And then he attended California State University Sacramento graduating with a Bachelor's Degree in Criminal Justice. While there he became exceedingly and intimately familiar with the surrounding neighborhoods. Folsom Blvd, East Sacramento areas are a stone's throw away. The American River with Campus Commons and a student population nearby. A little farther towards the hills and east he became familiar with the young couples residing near Mather Air Force Base. McClellan Air Force Base was also close.

When I was a child my father used to take us to the air shows at McClellan. Those are some of my happy memories. My dad had been stationed at Mather Air Force base coming to Sacramento from New York himself in the 1950's. He met my mother, married her and stayed in Sacramento after the Korean war. My older brother and I were both born at Mather. My mother used to throw all of us in the car in the wee hours of the morning to go pick my dad up from work at Mather driving us home to South Sacramento in the back of our 1963 Chevy Station Wagon.

## Monikers

Throughout this book there will be many times I will use the monikers many sleuths associated with the case already know. For those who have never read about the complicated use of many different names for this criminal the following is for you.

Visalia Ransacker............VR

The East Area Rapist........EAR

The Original Night Stalker .ONS

The Golden State Killer .....GSK

Law Enforcement.............LE

Joseph James DeAngelo .....JJD

## CHAPTER ONE

## The Crimes Known

**Visalia Ransacker Prior to becoming EAR/ONS**

What is ironic and crazy about the Visalia Ransacker series is that in the Exeter Police Department Joseph James DeAngelo was one of the officers assigned to the task of working the Burglary detail as shown in the article next page. DeAngelo was also the guy running amok in Visalia prowling and burglarizing homes to the tune of over 125 break-ins. Exeter was a ten-minute drive away from Visalia. Yet, no one was the wiser until after the Claude Snelling murder and after the investigation of the Visalia PD. Eventually they would come to Sacramento to talk about their case and the idea that Visalia thought EAR was the same man

Joseph DeAngelo moved to Exeter after an internship in Roseville PD landing there in 1973. He came to Exeter and lived there with his new wife. The article below shows the information and the time frame of JJD's involvement in the Exeter Burglary task force.

The CREEP Among Us * Anne Penn

## Police catch four youths

Through the investigative efforts of Exeter Police Officers Doug Cummings, Joe DeAngelo, Jerry Ellis, and Bob Long, four Exeter juveniles were arrested June 2 thus clearing two burglaries, a purse theft and a maliscious mischief incident.

Total recovery was made to the victim of one of the burglaries. Larry Johnson of Exeter received back property valued at $500 which included cameras, jewelry, shotguns, clock radios and a stereo receiver. Other victims of the crimes were Exeter Mercantile, burglary; Mohawk Gas Station, maliscious mischief; and Greta Willis, purse theft.

## DeAngelo's photograph when hired in Exeter, CA PD

Photo of Joseph James DeAngelo while he was an Exeter police officer.

The CREEP Among Us * Anne Penn

### Police officers foil two burglaries this week

Article for clarity: "Two attempted burglaries were foiled this past week by Exeter police officers.

On June 13 Office Joe DeAngelo observed a person attempting to break into a vehicle near the Fairway Apartments. DeAngelo pursued the suspect, who fled on foot, but failed to apprehend him. A slip wire was found in the right window of the vehicle by Sgt. Gary Fox and Officer Nick Cummings. The wire had been used to open the window of the auto owned by Steven George Gardiner, 310 North Orange. Nothing was taken from the car. While Sgt. Fox and Officer DeAngelo were on patrol duty the night of June 18 they observed that the door of the lube room of the Shell Station on Kaweah had been opened. A padlock had been cut off, but nothing had been taken from the station. Apparently the officers had frightened the wood be thief away." END OF ARTICLE

Another article in May talked about how the funds for an Anti-burglary task force were approved.

Composite Visalia Ransacker

**Simultaneously DeAngelo was doing the following:**

The Visalia Ransacker is a nickname given to a serial prowler, voyeur, burglar, and murderer who operated in Visalia, California in the mid-1970s. He is suspected to have committed around 120 crimes. In most of his crimes, the Ransacker would break into a single-family home and tear apart the interior while stealing only small items.

## The CREEP Among Us * Anne Penn

**Within the law enforcement community, it is believed that the Ransacker's crime spree began in March 1974 and ended in late 1975, the majority of his crimes having been committed near the College of the Sequoias. There is increasing evidence that the Ransacker moved away from Visalia shortly after he committed his only murder, then eventually became the East Area Rapist and the Original Night Stalker, now referred to as the Golden State Killer. In 2018, Joseph James DeAngelo was arrested as a suspect in the case, and was later charged with 1st degree murder. Wikipedia**

The first recorded ransacking was on Tuesday, March 19, 1974 when $50 of coins was stolen from a piggy-bank. Most of the Ransacker's activities involved breaking into houses, rifling through or vandalizing the owner's possessions, scattering women's underclothes, and stealing a range of low-value items, while often ignoring banknotes and higher valued items in plain sight. The Ransacker would also often arrange or display items in the house. Items emptied included piggy banks and coin-jars, and stolen items often included Blue Chip Stamps, foreign or historic coins, and personal items (such as single-earrings, cuff-links, rings, or medallions), but also included six weapons and various types of ammunition. Multiple same-day ransacking's were common as well, including 12 separate incidents on Saturday, November 30, 1974.

Common MOs of the burglaries included:

- scaling fences and moving through established routes such as parks, walkways, ditches, and trails
- attempting to pry open multiple points of entry, particularly windows
- leaving multiple points of escape open, especially windows as well as house, garage, and garden doors
- moving removed window screens onto beds or into bedrooms
- placing "warning items" such as dishes or bottles against doors and on door handles
- wearing gloves (given the absence of fingerprint evidence) Wikipedia

**Other crimes**]

It is possible that several earlier reported prowler and voyeur incidents in Visalia starting from mid-1973, an attempted rape on October 9, 1974, or a rape/kidnap on April 3, 1975, were also the work of the Ransacker Other similar burglaries and ransacking's in the Exeter area, dating from as far back as 1968 are also speculated to be connected based on MO similarities. Similarly, MO links are being made to the 1972-1973 crime spree of the 'Cordova Catburgler', and a couple of crimes after the McGowen attack may also be linked. There is also some speculation that other incidents, such as the deaths of Mt. Whitney High School students Jennifer Armour (aged 15; disappeared November 15, 1974;

found dead November 24, 1974) and Donna Richmond (aged 14; killed December 27, 1975), could also be related.

**Connection to the Golden State Killer**

Several months after the McGowen shooting, a prolific burglar and serial rapist, then called the East Area Rapist and now dubbed the Golden State Killer, began invading and attacking people in their homes roughly 200 miles (320 km) north in Sacramento County, California. Based on witness descriptions of the Rapist and the method of operation used to carry out his crimes, Detective McGowen attempted to link the Ransacker crimes to the sexual attacks in the Sacramento-area. Both the Ransacker and the Rapist were described as young-looking, physically fit white males in their twenties.

In terms of *modus operandi*, both the Ransacker and the Rapist pulled cold and hot prowl burglaries on single-story, detached homes in the middle of the night. Neither the Ransacker nor the Rapist took valuable items from the homes they burglarized, but often focused on personal items. Additionally, both the Ransacker and the Rapist carried and used firearms, both created multiple potential escape points by removing screens and unlocking/opening windows throughout the house, and both used items from within the household to create a series of alarms to detect movement. Both were also known to use stolen bicycles and local geography for movement. Both wore ski-masks and tennis shoes.

Based on such evidence, it is strongly suspected that the Ransacker and the Rapist are the same person. In all, the Ransacker is believed to be responsible for one murder and more than 100 burglaries in Visalia, while the Rapist/Killer committed 12 homicides, 51 rapes and more than 120 burglaries across California. However, unlike the Golden State Killer case, no current DNA link exists. In a 2017 interview, Contra Costa County DA cold case investigator Paul Holes was skeptical of the link between the two, based on credible witness descriptions, but upon identification of DeAngelo, he is now certain that the Golden State Killer was also the Visalia Ransacker.

**DeAngelo arrest**
*Main article: Golden State Killer § Joseph James DeAngelo*

Police made a breakthrough in the case on April 24, 2018, confirming that 72-year-old Citrus Heights resident Joseph James DeAngelo had been arrested and booked into the Sacramento County jail at approximately 2:30 a.m. on April 25 for two of the Original Night Stalker killings. During a news conference in Sacramento, Orange County District Attorney Tony Rackauckas stated that DeAngelo's case included suspected links to the Ransacker. It was also mentioned that DeAngelo had served as a police officer in nearby Exeter between May 19, 1973 and January 1976 before moving to Auburn. Fellow officers in Exeter at the time regarded him as a serious, aloof, and ambitious loner who may have actually ended up investigating some of his own crimes. His connection to the region may extend earlier than 1973, given that his sister is known to have moved to the area in 1969. Similarly, he is known to have trained at the College of the Sequoias prior to his time in Exeter.

A similar media session held by Visalia Chief of Police Jason Salazar confirmed that DeAngelo had served in Exeter during that time. Salazar stated that while there is no DNA linking DeAngelo to the Central Valley cases, his department has other evidence that will play a role in the investigation, and that he was "confident that the Visalia Ransacker has been captured." Though the statute of limitations for the burglaries have expired, DeAngelo was formally charged on August 13, 2018 with the 1st degree murder of Claude Snelling in 1975. END OF WIKIPEDIA INFORMATION

Article 3 years prior to JJD arrest

**Article from the Visalia Times Delta from 2015**

Is it possible that Visalia was the training ground, back in the 1970s, for one of California's most prolific serial-rapist/murderers? In a book that was recently published, "Hunting a Psychopath," author Richard Shelby states: "There are some who strongly believe he actually began his crime spree in 1974, in Visalia, California, where he was called the Visalia Ransacker." Shelby, who retired from the Sacramento Sheriff Department, was the original investigator of the East Area Rapist.

If you lived in Tulare County during the '70s, you may have the one piece of information that will solve Visalia's 100-plus home burglaries (along with the murder of a College of the Sequoias professor, Claude Snelling); Northern California's 50-plus rapes; and Goleta, Ventura, Irvine and Huntington

Beach's 12 known murders. The rapes in Northern California and the murders in Southern California have been linked by DNA. The questions remain: Did the suspect start in Visalia? Did he then commute or move to the Northern and Southern California locations? Did the Visalia Ransacker morph into the person known as the East Area Rapist/Original Night Stalker?

The Visalia Ransacker was described as approximately 5-foot, 9-inches, light-colored skin, short hair, size $9^1/_2$ shoe. On Dec. 10, 1975, during a neighborhood stakeout, the Ransacker pulled off a knit cap with his right hand, while pulling a revolver from his pocket with the other hand, at the same time saying, "Don't hurt me." He shot at Officer McGowen, hitting his flashlight. A composite drawing resulted from McGowen's description.

The East Area Rapist was described as approximately 5-foot, 9-inches, athletic build, late teen to 25, possibly ambidextrous with a tendency towards left hand, size $9-9^1/_2$ shoe, light-brown, shoulder-length hair worn in a semi-shag. A composite drawing of the EAR can be seen at *www.ear-ons.com*

The Visalia Ransacker ended his Visalia crime spree prior to the first known attack in Northern California, which happened in Ranch Cordova on June 18, 1976. However, the suspect may have been in the Sacramento area prior to this attack. Additional pictures, information, and timelines can once again be found: *www.ear-ons.com*

Please, if you have any ideas or information that may help, contact the Sacramento Sheriff's Department at 916-874-5057 or EARInfo@sacsheriff.com; Visalia's anonymous crime line at 559-734-5302, or the Santa Barbara Sheriff's Criminal Investigations Bureau at 805-681-4150.

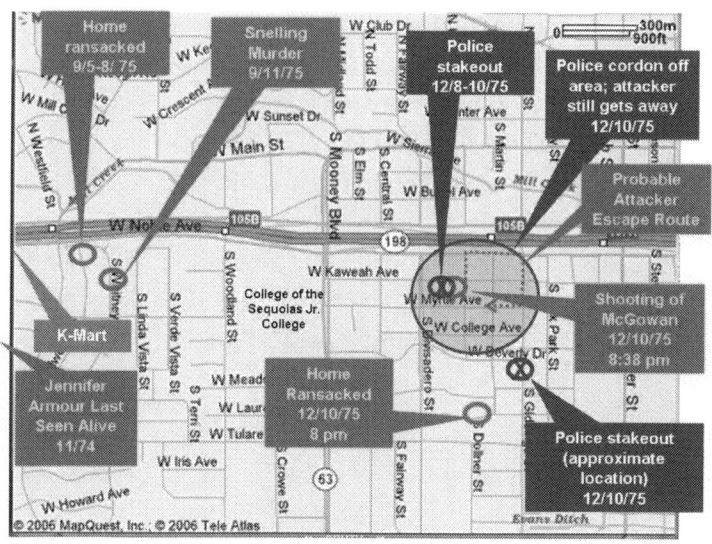

The following is what I wrote about and presented in my books previously. As it turns out Law Enforcement in their released redacted documents regarding the arrest of JJD also believe at long last that EAR is also VR. When we go back to the beginning of JJD's first actual employment as a police officer in Exeter it makes sense that he would have attacked and prowled in Visalia. It also makes sense that JJD would leave not long after the murder of Claude Snelling.

In speaking with a co-worker of JJD's from Exeter recently, Mr. Farrel Ward former officer and co-worker on August 27, 2018 here is what the discussion entailed:

Farrel Ward August 27, 2018

Mr. Ward at first screened my call, but picked up after I said who I was and my connection to the case. He must have wanted to talk and asked me why I wanted to know about what it was like working with DeAngelo. He asked me a couple of times if I was a reporter or something. I just want to know any detail about what happened and what people remember about JJD. I want to know for myself. I wanted to try to reconcile and determine how JJD was missed and allowed to continue on all those years ago.

As in many interviews already given Mr. Ward said JJD was just one of the guys and they were a very small department out in the country. 7-8 guys. Sounded like (and I resisted saying it) like a Mayberry type of police department. There is nothing wrong with that and I wish it was still that way more places.

He said no one could see anything weird about JJD, just that he was serious and did not smile. Said he "was smart, but had no common sense" also said that "he didn't know a joke"

I asked him about whether he was ever late for shifts or did not show up. He said he was always there and was on time. JJD worked with Mr. Ward sometimes in the patrol car. He would stop by his house and JJD would come in with him. I asked if he ever had him over or if his wife would come with him. He said no. Just couldn't leave him out in the car when he wanted to stop by his house (He said for a drink)

Mr. Ward also said he, JJD was too educated for the police force there. Told him he should go work for the FBI. I asked him if when JJD transferred if he seemed to be in a hurry at all. He said no. Once his transfer came through he gave two weeks' notice. We also talked about the murders that took place back then – he could not recall the names of the victims, but said what we all do and that is the cops should be looking into any connections on those.

I asked Mr. Ward if he thought it was weird that no one knew JJD was breaking and entering since he was in charge or worked on the burglary task force. He said well JJD knew how much time he had, how long it would take for cops to respond to a call. Knew what to do and what not to leave as evidence. I said the composite of the guy McGowen described looked the most like JJD and he agreed. He also said he thought the composite McGowen helped with was the only one that really looked like JJD. He said when he heard the name Joseph DeAngelo he thought it must be a guy who had the same name not truly the man he had worked with. Then he saw the picture of JJD after the arrest and knew immediately it was the same guy he had worked with so long ago, but older of course.

Mr. Ward mentioned that JJD had a sister who lived not far from him now. Said she was married and had a daughter also still living in Exeter.

Mr. Ward did not seem to have the story straight about Bonnie. I filled him in on that. I told him about when I was chased and he said I was lucky to have not been one of JJD victims. He had asked me a couple of times if I was a victim although I told him I was Lyman Smith's niece. Mr. Ward did not know all of the detail in the cases as there is so much to know, but he did know Lyman was an attorney. He said he was sorry that JJD did so many horrible things to so many people. When I told him about the bludgeoning of Lyman he offered his apology (condolences) Seems like a nice guy. He tried to be helpful and to help me understand how JJD was missed in Exeter. I do understand how JJD did not set off any alarm bells there.

When I told him about being chased he said it was too bad I did not have a gun. I did tell him about moving away from Sacramento in 1984 because I did not feel safe. He said that was probably a very good idea at the time.

So the bottom line unless another co-worker has anything to say is there was nothing that triggered any kind of awareness that JJD was strange or creepy in any way. There was nothing that made anyone think he was doing anything wrong when he was not there. He always came to work and always was on time.

I think JJD made himself as benign as he could and had the ability to fit in on purpose. He had to have laughed his butt off because Exeter had no idea and obviously Visalia had no idea that the guy was an officer. Visalia knew he was the same guy as EAR in Sacramento a couple of years later, but never looked at any of the very few officers they had 10 minutes away during the crimes of VR.

Mr. Ward said that the Visalia Ransacker knew it would take 10-15 minutes and as long as 30 minutes for cops to show up for the burglaries because they were in the country. The Ransacker was always long gone when the cops arrived and there was no evidence left behind. That in itself would have made me wonder if it was a cop. The perp knew what to do and not do. Why? I would have asked myself. How could he NEVER be caught with over 125 burglaries in the area? How could he never be caught when he himself was on the burglary task force and when JJD himself had been investigating his own burglaries and prowling's now and again? It must have been difficult for him to keep a straight face and not laugh as he interviewed his own victims. Except we know JJD had no sense of humor and we know he did not smile – at least while he worked for the Exeter police department.

I sure would love to have been able to read the police reports he wrote about the Ransacking's that he himself had committed. Hindsight is 20/20.

Did not know anything, did not see anything, did not suspect anything. Short story. Which explains how DeAngelo was able to just walk away. Did they not think it odd that the Visalia Ransacker just vanished about the same time JJD did? No they did not. There was no reason to suspect JJD at that time. I hope to ask that question of the Visalia police detectives who are still with us.

**And so what follows is what I had written and thought previously in Murder on His Mind Serial Killer about the Visalia Ransacker and if he could be the same guy:**

"I could not ignore the activities of the Visalia Ransacker and the at length discussion Richard Shelby has written about in his book. I have a hard time thinking of VR as a separate individual from EAR and ONS. I truly believe the prowling's and ransacking in Visalia could have been committed by the same individual known as the East Area Rapist. In 1974 this guy had to be between 19 and 25. My belief is that he was more likely 19. I think he could have relatives in the area of Visalia as he graduated from high school in approximately 1972 or 1973. This gave him the freedom to go stay wherever he pleased. Once again I am speculating as I believe this is how the story went. I am entitled to my opinion.

"The reason I want to discuss this chapter of the criminals' wanderings is because there are similarities to point out and also because I believe if VR and EAR are the same guy he was in training for what was to come. He was developing his prowling patterns, he was discovering what he liked, what excited him and he was deciding how he could be successful in this line of work as it were. He certainly did not receive any great pay out monetarily or from things he would randomly take. His payoff came in learning his craft and in the excitement and satisfaction he got from figuring out how he would be successful as a burglar. I could be wrong. If he always had murder on his mind I think this could be how he began and how he worked to become EAR and then ONS. I think he thought it was fun to see what he could get away with. He knew he was fast on his feet. He knew he could jump fences and run away into the night. He knew how not to call attention to himself. He was organized and methodical about what he did minimizing the risk to himself. He realized early on that it worked best if he were to enter residences ahead of time looking for weapons and anything that could take him by surprise, harm him or kill him. He also decided that attacking women alone would also minimize his risk.

I am thinking he was practicing breaking and entering in a community that was smaller than a city and that had easy escapes. This guy as I have stated before was studying and schooling himself on how to be the ultimate outlaw. I truly believe that he wanted to be extremely prepared for what he was about to do next. Breaking in and raping women.

This guy was logical practiced, and ready when he raped in Sacramento for the first time. It must have been a most exhilarating high for him to do it and get away with it. It was an adrenaline rush never before experienced. So, I tend to lean towards the

Visalia Ransacker being the same guy as EAR. The timeline fits, and there are several similarities in his MO. I think the guy graduated from high school in 1973 or 72. I think he set about learning his trade as an outlaw soon after his graduation. I also think that these types of crimes could possibly have been what he tried to do as a teenager in his own neighborhood and then thought better of it. He moved out of the range of his home. "

On September 11, 1975, Claude Snelling, a journalism professor at the College of the Sequoias in Visalia was shot while trying to stop an intruder from kidnapping his daughter in the middle of the night. Professor Snelling was killed. In December of the same year a detective on stakeout where traces of a prowler had been found attempted to arrest a masked man. The suspect got away because he feigned surrender and then shot at the officer. The prowler escaped before a cordon was established in the area. After this incident and barely getting away the burglary spree stopped in Visalia. A few months later the soon to be East Area Rapist began attacks in Sacramento.

By the time the perpetrator started the rapes in Sacramento he was very well practiced. There were over 125 crimes in Visalia over the time span of April 6, 1974 until December 10, 1975. VR loved the rush he got from breaking and entering. Six months would go by before the first reported rape in Sacramento June 18, 1976". END OF QUOTE FROM MY PREVIOUS BOOKS MURDER ON HIS MIND

## Police Seeking To Link Rapist, Snelling Slayer
*Visalia Times-Delta*, 18 May 1977, By Miles Shuper - **ARTICLE**

Two Visalia police detectives are in Sacramento today probing the possibility that a man being sought as a suspect in the raping of 23 women could be the Visalia Ransacker and possibly the killer of Claude Snelling.

A number of similarities in physical description and actions of the Sacramento rapist and the Visalia ransacker have swung the Visalia investigation, the most intensive in the city's history, to the state's capital city. Although it has never been proved, investigators have been working on the premise that the ransacker is the same person who killed the College of Sequoias journalism instructor Sept. 11, 1975.

Lt. Roy Springmeyer said today, "Because of the degree of the similarity in the physical descriptions and the methods used, we just can't afford to overlook the possibility that the same person could be responsible for the rapes and the Visalia crimes."

Detectives Bill McGowen and Duane Shipley left Visalia early today to meet in Sacramento with investigators probing the rapes in which the attacker now has threatened to kill two persons. The increasing violent behavior of the Sacramento attacker matches the psychological profile compiled during investigation of the Visalia Ransacker case and the murder of Snelling, investigators said.

In the Sacramento case, psychologists believe the rapist is trying to prove himself sexually because he "has difficulty establishing a normal sexual relationship."

When psychologists compiled a profile of the man responsible for the Visalia crimes, they said he probably would become more violent and dangerous.

Officers also are convinced that the man who shot Snelling is the man who shot at Detective McGowen during a Dec. 10 stakeout of a neighborhood in which a prowler, believed to be the Ransacker, had been working. McGowen was not hurt, but a bullet pierced the veteran officer's flashlight. It was between the time of the Snelling murder and the shot fired at the officer that the string of Sacramento rapes began, generally in October, 1975.

Visalia investigators said the first Sacramento rapes during late 1975 could have been committed by the man sought in the Visalia cases. In Sacramento the frequency of the rapes has been increasing along with the degree of violence. In recent weeks the rapist has become increasing bold and on six occasions the sexual attacks were committed after the victims' husbands were tied up by the attacker. In most of the earlier attacks, however, the victim was alone in the home. The rapist typically wears a mask, ties up people and ransacks the house.
The Sacramento attacks have occurred in middle-income and upper-income residential areas and a

local group calling itself the east Area Rapist Surveillance Patrol is offering a $10,000 reward for the arrest and conviction of the rapist.

In Visalia $4,000 is being offered for the arrest and conviction of Snelling's killer. Visalia police Sgt. John Vaughan who has been heading the Snelling murder investigation said today he has copies of many of the Sacramento rape investigation reports and the profiles of the crime patterns.

They are being closely studied and compared to the information gathered by Visalia officers during the 20-month investigation of the Visalia slaying and the nearly four-year probe of the ransacking burglaries, Vaughan said. There also are similarities of the composite pictures of the Snelling-ransacker suspect and the Sacramento rapist.

The Visalia subject is described as between 25 and 30 years of age, 5-foot, 10 inches in height and 180 to 200 pounds in weight. He was described as having short, straight blond hair, a pale smooth round face and stubby feet and hands. The subject is believed to be left handed, and often wore a dark ski mask.

The subject in the Sacramento cases is described as between 19 and 30 years of age with blue or hazel eyes, five-foot eight to 10 inches in height, with a "good build" and dirty blond or medium brown hair. The Sacramento rapist also wears a ski mask.

In Sacramento during a news conference, Fred Reese, chief deputy sheriff said "This individual is probably in a homosexual panic caused by his inadequate endowment." Reese said the rapist, who

typically carries a gun or and a knife but has never disfigured or wounded any victim, probably had a "domineering" mother and an "absent" father or a weak father. Reese based his comments of reports of psychologists and psychiatrists who have studied all known facts about the rapist.
**END OF ARTICLE**

**My comments now:** Law Enforcement appeared to be on the right track back in 1977 when this article came out. One of the things that stands out to me in this report is the fact that a psychological profile was done by the Visalia police department after the murder of Claude Snelling in 1975. In the psychological profile it is mentioned that the increasingly violent behavior of the Sacramento attacker matches their criminal. This article came out May 18, 1977. In Sacramento during this time frame there were at least 5 attacks, one May 3, one May 5, one on May 14, one on May 17 and one May 28, all in the Sacramento area. Then the attacks stopped until September right after labor day 1977. Labor day was September 5 that year. The attack in Stockton came immediately after the holiday weekend on Tuesday September 6. The summer must have required more hours at work or something else requiring his attention during the summer months.

Also of note were the comments made in the last paragraph of the article by Fred R, a chief deputy sheriff about the perpetrator. Because we are relatively certain JJD read all the news about his crimes, his story, these statements were very inflammatory and likely really made JJD rage.

Where the chief deputy formed his opinions about the perp being in a homosexual panic one has to remember the times in which the comments were made. In the 70's many stereotypes and social labels and constraints were made. Still the comments likely really made the criminal very angry.

## The LA Times and Sacramento UPI picked up this story on July 23, 1978

## Headlines were Sacramento's 'East Area Rapist' May Be Visalia Killer

Sacramento (UPI) – Authorities are investigating whether the notorious East Area Rapist in Sacramento is a man known to Visalia police as The Ransacker and a murderer, the Sacramento Union reported Saturday.

The East Area Rapist, named for his attacks primarily in the eastern suburbs of Sacramento, has assaulted nearly 40 women and teenagers since October, 1975. Some of his attacks have occurred outside the city, in Davis and Stockton areas.

The Ransacker committed more than 125 ransacking burglaries in Visalia during the early 1970's and is believed to have shot and killed a journalism instructor who tried to stop the Ransacker from abducting his teen age daughter, the paper said. END OF ARTICLE

## My comments now:

As we can see, as early as 1977 there was an article in the Sacramento Bee reporting that there was a possibility that the Visalia Ransacker was the East Area Rapist. Authorities discussed the possible connection more than once between 1977 and 1980 and possibly beyond that time frame. It appears that the idea was discounted or dismissed each time. The story I have heard about Visalia PD being blown off by Sacramento PD is Visalia was told they were just seeking publicity. Another article from 2015:

## The CREEP Among Us * Anne Penn

Is it possible that Visalia was the training ground, back in the 1970s, for one of California's most prolific serial-rapist/murderers? In a book that was recently published, "Hunting a Psychopath," author Richard Shelby states: "There are some who strongly believe he actually began his crime spree in 1974, in Visalia, California, where he was called the Visalia Ransacker." Shelby, who retired from the Sacramento Sheriff Department, was the original investigator of the East Area Rapist.

If you lived in Tulare County during the '70s, you may have the one piece of information that will solve Visalia's 100-plus home burglaries (along with the murder of a College of the Sequoias professor, Claude Snelling); Northern California's 50-plus rapes; and Goleta, Ventura, Irvine and Huntington Beach's 12 known murders. The rapes in Northern California and the murders in Southern California have been linked by DNA. The questions remain: Did the suspect start in Visalia? Did he then commute or move to the Northern and Southern California locations? Did the Visalia Ransacker morph into the person known as the East Area Rapist/Original Night Stalker?

The Visalia Ransacker was described as approximately 5-foot, 9-inches, light-colored skin, short hair, size $9^1/_2$ shoe. On Dec. 10, 1975, during a neighborhood stakeout, the Ransacker pulled off a knit cap with his right hand, while pulling a revolver from his pocket with the other hand, at the same time saying, "Don't hurt me." He shot at Officer McGowen, hitting his flashlight. A composite drawing resulted from McGowen's description.

The CREEP Among Us * Anne Penn

The East Area Rapist was described as approximately 5-foot, 9-inches, athletic build, late teen to 25, possibly ambidextrous with a tendency towards left hand, size 9-9$^1/_2$ shoe, light-brown, shoulder-length hair worn in a semi-shag. A composite drawing of the EAR can be seen at *www.ear-ons.com*

The Visalia Ransacker ended his Visalia crime spree prior to the first known attack in Northern California, which happened in Ranch Cordova on June 18, 1976. However, the suspect may have been in the Sacramento area prior to this attack. Additional pictures, information, and timelines can once again be found: *www.ear-ons.com*

Please, if you have any ideas or information that may help, contact the Sacramento Sheriff's Department at 916-874-5057 or EARInfo@sacsheriff.com; Visalia's anonymous crime line at 559-734-5302, or the Santa Barbara Sheriff's Criminal Investigations Bureau at 805-681-4150.

A copy of "Hunting a Psychopath" recently was donated to the Tulare County Public Library or can be ordered online. END OF ARTICLE

M.J. Smith lives in Visalia

http://www.visaliatimesdelta.com/story/opinion/2015/03/25/visalia-training-ground/70406130/

As of 2017 all of the above phone numbers and contact information are correct and can be used to speak with Law Enforcement.

**Update**: Joseph James DeAngelo is believed to also be the Visalia Ransacker. Mr. DeAngelo has been charged in the 1975 murder of Professor Claude Snelling in Visalia as of August 2018

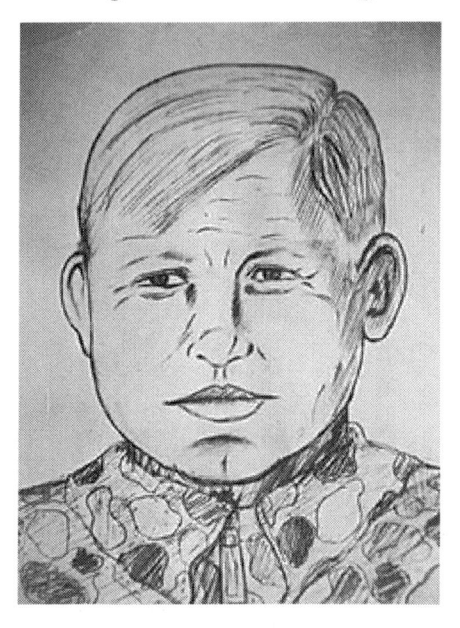

. In my opinion this composite looked the most like DeAngelo during the Visalia Ransacker series. Officer McGowen who was shot by VR saw the perpetrator without his mask briefly. The criminal lost weight apparently as he moved to Auburn not long after this composite was put out into the community of Visalia as the possible murder suspect of Claude Snelling. Over time as the years went by there were many in Law Enforcement and elsewhere that debated over and over about whether or not the

Visalia Ransacker was the same guy in Sacramento that had escalated to rape. Paul Holes was a nonbeliever. He did not see a connection. Debates went on and on everywhere. Many in Law Enforcement did not see the connection. Some did. I also have to state here that DeAngelo gave his two week notice sometime after the murder of Claude Snelling and after the shooting of McGowen .DeAngelo had outsmarted both Exeter PD and Visalia PD as he knew working out of Exeter the Visalia PD would be none the wiser as DeAngelo turned in his two week notice in Exeter and left the area that his departure would not cause any red flags anywhere at all. DeAngelo had applied for and gotten a job back in his old stomping grounds. Auburn, CA.

### Profile statement from Leslie D'Ambrosia written sometime after 1986

"The fact that the killer attacked his victims inside their homes is significant. The few serial killers that have been known to attack inside the victims' residences proved to have histories of committing burglaries. In these four cases, the offender also was able to enter in a stealth manner without alerting his victims. Based on these facts we would surmise that your offender would likely be an accomplished cat burglar"

Sometime after 1986 the profile written by Leslie D'Ambrosia had the above comment included in it. Many definitely thought the offender was a burglar and that he was very accomplished at that endeavor. Connecting the cat burglar from the Visalia crimes and then tracking him to Sacramento as he became

### The CREEP Among Us * Anne Penn

EAR we should truly have known as the Visalia PD seemed to know back in 1977 that the man was the same guy Hindsight throughout after the fact.

## CHAPTER TWO

## More Crimes

Let me back up and tell you about the crimes of this alleged criminal whose DNA matches the evidence left at the crime scenes all those years ago....

Because there were at least 50 rapes and 13 murders one could just write about the attacks which were scary, dehumanizing and of course many. I do not want to call attention to his many crimes one by one. Others have documented in detail what exactly this perpetrator did in order to terrorize and eventually kill so many. What I will add here so that one can know as much as is possible just how terrible these crimes were I will tell about some of the peeping, stalking and then rapes starting from the beginning.

If you have not read other books that tell how this criminal was one of the worst we have encountered along the way I will attempt to give a snapshot of his evil. There have been many evil monsters out there since when I became aware of them in the 1960's. Many, many of them have been apprehended and are serving time mostly forever in various penitentiary's. John Wayne Gacy died in prison, Dahmer was killed by another inmate in prison. Son of Sam is still in prison where he will remain. Sirhan, Sirhan, Mark David Chapman are both still in prison. Chapman was recently denied parole for about the 10th time.

These were all murderers and each had different motivations for their crimes. Each type of killer or killings were motivated and came from a different place of rage. The two women, Leslie Van Houten and Patricia Krenwinkle who were originally sentenced to die for the murders dictated by Charles Manson still remain in prison having their sentences commuted to life back in the 70's.

BTK had to call attention to himself one more time in about 2004 and was apprehended using DNA from a family member to tell him they knew that his daughter was related to BTK. The Green River Killer Gary Ridgeway is incarcerated having killed at least 49 women in the state of Washington. The Zodiac is still on the loose unless he has died since his crimes in the Bay Area in the late 1960's. Possibly DNA will be able to tell us at last who the Zodiac is and soon. But, finally we have the guy responsible who we have called the Visalia Ransacker, The East Area Rapist and the Original Night Stalker. He had no other names until the last couple of years. Joseph James DeAngelo is behind bars in Sacramento County. The last moniker was added very recently which everyone has given in to namely, The Golden State Killer. So many people across the state and then across the nation had never heard of this killer by any name until recently.

This was a case that no one was really talking about until about 2001, 2004 and 2010. In 2010 former Lieutenant Larry Crompton from the Contra Costa County Rape Task Force wrote a book detailing the cases of the East Area Rapist, Original Night Stalker calling it Sudden Terror. He wanted to document as best he could the crimes of this man who had remained unidentified and free all of these years.

And then it was announced in 2016 that the FBI was finally going to reopen the case. The next 2 years were flooded with information to bring the country up to speed with what we in Sacramento, Visalia, Stockton, Walnut Creek, Modesto, Fresno and the list goes on dealt with. The many, many jurisdictions the man crossed into from 1973 until 1986 were familiar with this beast. Starting as a peeper, prowler, burglar he progressed to become a murderer by 1975. As the Visalia Ransacker he broke into Claude Snelling's residence and tried to abduct his daughter Beth Snelling, age 16. As he tried to drag her out of her home her father heard the commotion. Confronting the would be abductor Beth's father was shot twice while the perp fled. Mr. Snelling died on the way to the hospital.

VR murdered for self-preservation and to keep his freedom in the beginning. He murdered again in 1978 when he was known as EAR killing Brian and Katie Maggiore a newly married young couple who had seen his face. Chasing them down and killing them in cold blood in Rancho Cordova California February 2, 1978.

The fact remains that all of these criminals known to us before the 1970's, during the 1970's and later on during our lifetimes possessed the mindset to kill

The CREEP Among Us * Anne Penn

people who had the right to live. All of the murderers had many different issues that drove them to kill, drove them to be evil. All deserved punishment. The 72-year-old man named Joseph James DeAngelo, alleged killer who is sitting in the Sacramento County jail currently and for only the last 150 plus days is the personification of evil and what is the worst a human being can be. Partly because he was assigned to protect us as a police officer. He was a Navy Officer who again was assigned to protect us during the Vietnam War.

He most likely was drafted to protect our country in some way during those most rotten of times, but I believe he was likely most willing to go and was wanting to go. I say this because he already knew what his path was to be. He knew the military would teach him skills he would later need and use against us. All of society and all of our communities would be victim to the knowledge he would learn and possess. Later as he was released from the military he went to school obtaining skills in police science and criminal justice, criminal law. He was a good student. He acquired an internship in the Roseville Police Department in what would turn out to be once again his old neck of the woods. DeAngelo applied to be an officer with the Exeter Police Department in 1973. He could hardly wait to begin his crimes.

In 1973 Joseph James DeAngelo was hired as a police officer. He became the Visalia Ransacker

After graduating from California State University in Sacramento with a degree in Criminal Justice JJD was hired in May 1973 on the Exeter police force which is about ten minutes away from Visalia, CA. The DeAngelo's did not start a family until eight years passed. His wife was still attending classes in order to become a lawyer. The DeAngelo's lived in Exeter, CA from 1973 until 1976.

DeAngelo was involved on the burglary task force and ironically the Visalia Ransacker began prowling, and breaking and entering residences in Visalia, CA during the entire time DeAngelo was on the Exeter police force. The Visalia Ransacker was able to tally at least 125 burglaries and never was caught.

In September 1975 a prowler broke into the home of Claude Snelling while everyone in the home was asleep. I have added the articles detailing this crime in another chapter, but the bottom line is that the intruder broke in, attacked Beth Snelling who was 16 at the time and began to drag her from her home. Her father heard the commotion and ran to try and save his daughter. The intruder shot Mr. Snelling twice. He then kicked Beth in the face and disappeared. Mr. Snelling died on the way to the hospital. Shortly after this murder the Visalia police department set up a sting in the area hoping to catch the guy known as the Visalia Ransacker. Detective McGowen did stop a man with a mask. The prowler played a farce about giving up and then tried to shoot McGowen. The shot hit McGowen's flashlight breaking and splintering glass into the detective's eye. The intruder had taken off his mask in order to stall the detective so his face was briefly seen. In the commotion the Visalia Ransacker slipped away. A composite was drawn and shown to the public.

Not long after this incident, DeAngelo applied for a position with the Auburn Police Department. It was now the end of 1975. JJD was hired on in Auburn beginning in May 1976. In the meantime, the attacks and break-ins stopped in Visalia. The attacks, prowling's and rapes began in Sacramento mostly in the east part of town in June 1976. Not much time went by between when he began his new job in Auburn and the first known attacks in East Sacramento.

In retrospect and because hindsight truly is 20/20 I have to say that in writing the facts of the story as they played out, showing how DeAngelo was in the areas from Visalia to Sacramento to Southern, CA it is difficult to tell how easy it might have been to track this guy IF Law Enforcement had just talked to one another in Exeter and Visalia in 1975. Later on in discussions as the story unfolded we know the Visalia detectives did come to Sacramento to discuss the possibilities of Visalia Ransacker being EAR. Old fashioned police work would have indicated that the Visalia Ransacker did move on in 1975. Visalia Police did know VR had moved on. Exeter Police Departments also knew JJD had moved on and they knew specifically where he had gone. They did notice the man named EAR in Sacramento. They did try to compare notes and share information within two years of the Snelling murder. The composite they had IF they had looked at Exeter and Visalia personnel in the police departments might have indicated that one of their own officers could be the perp. The burglary task force in Exeter had DeAngelo working on it at the time. I will stop at this point and move on as you can read about all of this in the clipped articles I have included in this book. The trail was right in front of them yet DeAngelo really did know that these agencies did not and would not communicate from each town (County) with one another. He knew.

It was not ever really about how smart DeAngelo was or how lucky he was it was about how the system worked and did not work and it was about the fact that DeAngelo knew where the weaknesses were. It was calculated, studied and executed. And so in fact as it turns out DeAngelo really was smart. Smarter than the system he had studied.

## Chapter Three

## Auburn

## May 1976 – July 1979

How did the CREEP do this? It was easy. When JJD transferred to Auburn PD and also while he lived there he traveled at night down Auburn Folsom Road which is the back way to get to East Sacramento and Citrus Heights. He could use this road anytime and be fairly sure no one would notice him. No one would notice his comings and goings. If he worked at night, he could actually be on shift as he drove his squad car to the areas. I am pretty certain he never drove his squad car there, but what would stop him from picking up a different car to drive the roads and back? JJD was fairly certain he would not encounter anyone on those back roads in 1976 especially between eleven and five a.m.

Most people would drive the I-80 West to Roseville and to Citrus Heights simply because it is a highway. But, by going the back roads starting in Auburn, it was time efficient as well as a more private way to get to his target areas unnoticed. One can take Auburn Folsom Road all the way from Auburn to Folsom and into Citrus Heights. I do talk about this on my maps in another chapter. Back in the day because this was so rural no one would really see JJD as he either left work after his shift to create terror in Sacramento and no one would see the car he would pick to drive. Auburn Folsom was sort of tucked between Highway 49 and Highway 80. Highway 49 would take too long and is too curvy. The only time I could see JJD taking that road would be if he attacked in the Placerville area or in the gold hills of Coloma or in any small town along that route. It is my opinion though that JJD preferred Auburn Folsom Road. I would have. I used to drive it when I lived in Roseville off Cirby Way and I also would drive that way to get to Auburn on one of my many treks there as a young woman. My first husband and I would go there to hike, swim in the river and then have the best Mexican food at the D's Mexican restaurant. This little hole in the wall is in Old Auburn existing in a very old building which was likely built in about 1850 during the Gold Rush in California. Many old buildings still grace the landscape there which is why I was attracted to its old time charm. Old Victorian's sit on the hills, a gigantic sculpture of a gold panning miner still sits near the entrance to the town.

The old courthouse sits high on top of a hill, the color of the old building matching the beautiful sunsets one can see every night. Even after all of these years Auburn feels the way it did in the 1970's. JJD did not take that away from the town. I do not feel him there. What I found there recently is what I remember. I took the same hike down near the river near the old railroad bridge. There was no creep there no bad vibes. Just amazement from me that the CREEP we know, the evil, evil man was a borrower of space and time, especially there. He worked and lived there and it turned out to be the perfect place to move from there out on the old rural roads over and over again creeping up into unsuspecting neighborhoods in East Sacramento. In Citrus Heights. It was the easiest and simplest of plans which is why it worked and why he was not caught. He almost screwed it up because he thought he could steal from a store, cocky and arrogant he almost screwed up his plans. That will come later.

JJD worked in the small building in the Auburn police department. On the right side is the parking lot and in the back and on the left side is a fenced in yard where the squad cars live. From the parking lot a cop could always see two crosses above the church. He could see right across the street and out of the front window there is a church named St. Joseph's Catholic Church. He could even see the interstate signs and hop on the I-80 freeway if he had desired to in order to move quickly to Roseville, it is only about 16 miles. But, that would have him travelling at late hours on a major freeway when no one would be out there but him. So, he took the Auburn Folsom road. Perfect.

Next to the police station is ironically, a car lot and car repair and service area. There are many cars there and even some for sale. Would it have been difficult to take a car, a different car for each mission he had in mind? Was he friends or acquainted with the people who owned it back then? Seemed so convenient. Was JJD able to access the property and did he? Did he use the keys hanging on the rack inside the dealership from the cars that were for sale? They were used cars. He would probably laugh to himself each time he took the keys, started a car and drove away. It would seem so easy and right under everyone's nose. Totally in keeping with his brazenness, his bold and arrogant style. I would bet JJD worked the three to eleven shift. Got off and left with any car he wanted. No one at the station would know especially if he walked across the street, took a key, took a car and brought it back before the next shift change at 7:00 a.m. the next morning. No cameras, no noise and no one watching. The car dealership used to be a Dodge dealership and repair. It has been there butted up against and across the street from the Police Station for the last sixty years.

Both corners of the street are occupied by the dealership. Like I said, no cameras in the 70's, no surveillance. Another absolutely perfect fit for JJD. If JJD worked day shift he could take off at night and go anywhere. Arriving back home catching a few hours of sleep before working again. If he worked the three to eleven shift even better as he would get off at night, drive to Fair Oaks and Citrus Heights, Rancho Cordova all accessible easily. In as little as 19 minutes after terrorizing the good people in East Sacramento JJD could arrive back in Auburn, no one would know, no one did know.

While I investigated these crimes and these places prior to JJD's arrest I had begun to look into how JJD travelled without detection. I had started looking at a place called Rio Vista. Rio Vista has access to roads out in the country that easily hooked up to the freeway system. A small town, it is located South West from Sacramento. It would have been easy to travel, no one would have noticed him, yet the town was so close to I-80 and his travels down South, this was where I had begun to look for him. I told Larry Crompton my thoughts, I told Mark. I even ran across some tourists from Rio Vista and we talked about the East Area Rapist. They too remembered him and the stories. I worked with Mark in different areas tracking another person of interest to see if he had ties to that area and then to relatives in Southern CA. This POI had a brother and two sisters. His profession also LE. I had travelled to Sacramento April 24 to gather trash from a sister for DNA testing. We were on the right track when it came to searching in small towns surrounding Sacramento. Sooner or later I would have gone north. I had been focused on the Highway connection to Southern CA which is why Rio Vista was my focus in 2018. An easy on and off, remote, kicked back, small town population, much like Auburn in that way.

Auburn police station from the parking lot

In back and around to the fence are the police cars – there are two gates – one on each side

## The CREEP Among Us * Anne Penn

The CREEP Among Us * Anne Penn

View from the Police Station parking lot

## The CREEP Among Us * Anne Penn

This is the pleasant scene directly behind the police station

Behind the police station down from the parking lot

To the right behind the parking lot it is now an open place with picnic tables. This area was redone to return to a more natural landscaped area in the 1990's after JJD had long ago left the area.

But what it tells us is that this was an open area, complete with a stream, paths and not too unlike areas that JJD preferred in his travels.

Also part of what is now behind the police station, Auburn, CA

The CREEP Among Us * Anne Penn

Auburn Police Station

Auburn Police Department, front door where JJD could enter. Likely cops on duty had a separate entrance from the public, but it is not farfetched to think he came and went here as well.

Just down the street from the police station is the church I was married in May 1980. The vestibule of the church where my grandfather Lyman Senior sobbed and sobbed after my wedding in Auburn 8 weeks after the murder of his son Lyman Smith and daughter-in-law, Charlene Smith.

Here is that story:

"In February 1980 I was 23 years old. I had become engaged on Valentine's Day. My future husband and I set about planning our wedding. In March 1980 my grandfather's son Lyman Robert Smith was murdered. After this fact began to sink in my grandmother's reaction at first was that there was no way they could come to my wedding. It had been planned for May 10, 1980 a mere 8 weeks since Lyman Senior had learned that his oldest son was dead. A mere eight weeks since he was told all of the gruesome details about how his son and his wife had been murdered.

## The CREEP Among Us * Anne Penn

I can still recall my grandfather's words when faced with the idea of not attending my wedding. He said "Of course we will be there." We have to be there, and then they offered their punch bowl to use at my reception. Somehow Lyman Smith Senior found the strength along with my grandmother Veonia to come to my wedding in May 1980. They did not want us to postpone it, but wanted to move forward.

The last time my grandfather had sat in a church it was March 22, 1980 along with 350 other people to listen as the Rev. Leonard Dixon eulogized Lyman Robert and Charlene Smith. Somehow this man sat through my wedding listening to my cousins' sing as the rain came down on the roof of the church on this day. The wedding was in a beautiful old church in Auburn, California. After I walked with my new husband back down the aisle having just been married, in the vestibule my grandmother and grandfather were standing there. My grandfather was sobbing and sobbing and sobbing. He could not be consoled. He could not stop crying. There was nothing anyone could do for him. No one knew what to do. Somehow Lyman Senior managed to get to his car and drive my grandmother to my reception in Roseville."

Vestibule of the Auburn church I was married in (right around the corner from the police station)

The CREEP Among Us * Anne Penn

Inside the Pioneer United Methodist Church where I was married May 1980

Pioneer United Methodist Church

The church I was married in May 10, 1980 which is a short distance from the police station and Highway 80.

It is the oldest church in Placer County, built in 1854.

Court house just down the street from the church I was married in and also just down the street from the police station.

Court house on the hill

Old Town Auburn, CA an old Livery Stable turned art gallery

Not far from this sign one can hop on the Auburn Folsom Road

Gold panner sculpture across from Highway 80 and an entrance to Highway 80.

The CREEP Among Us * Anne Penn

To the right you can see the railroad tracks that run over I-80. This is the Gold Panning sculpture made by Dr. Ken Fox.

## The CREEP Among Us * Anne Penn

Landmarks in Old Downtown Auburn

The CREEP Among Us * Anne Penn

Landmarks in Auburn

Not far from Auburn Ravine Road this is downtown Auburn. Even today it seems frozen in time.

Car lot which butts up against the fence shared by Auburn Police Department – this was taken October 5, 2018

It was used for the same purpose in 1976-1979 when JJD was there

Current dealership has nothing to do with crimes from 42 years ago. The dealership building has been there and functioned as a dealership which included used cars for the last 60 years It occupies the corner across the street also

The CREEP Among Us * Anne Penn

Lots of used cars parked here sharing the same fence as the Police Department next door

91

St. Joseph's Catholic Church right across the street from the Police Station and also across from the Highway 80 On Ramp.

Left side front of building as one stands in front of the Auburn Police Station. Alley to where police cars are parked.

The fence on the left butts up against the car dealership that has been there for 60 years

Top: The view of St. Joseph's from the police station Auburn, CA Bottom: Front of police station

Right drive takes one to the parking lot. Left side was on previous photo where police cars are kept and next door to car dealership

Taken from the sidewalk in front of the station

Highway 80 on ramp is right across the street

If one designed a way for a serial killer who began as a serial rapist and killer to get around undetected this story is the perfect one.

The CREEP Among Us * Anne Penn

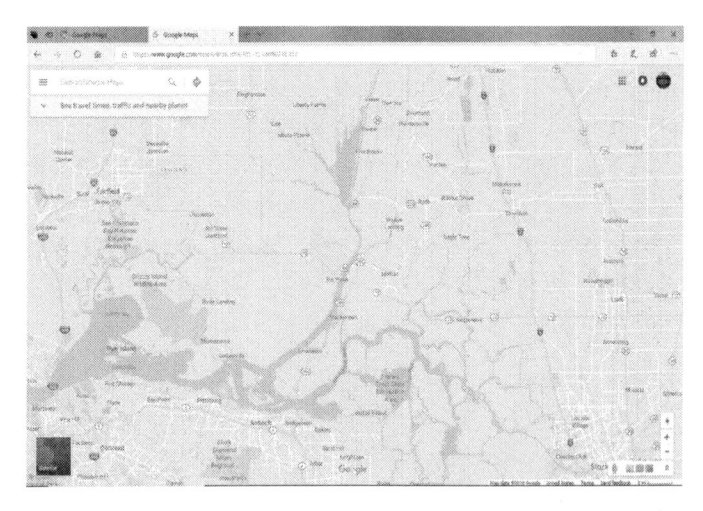

Map showing the highway connections South West of Sacramento Rio Vista, Highway 12, Highway 99, Highway 80

To 680 and others and the easy frontage roads that would connect to easy highway on and off access

Google map Rio Vista yourself and also trace Highway 99 South to Stockton and other places JJD went

In a conversation I had with Nick Willick previous Police Chief from Auburn, CA this is what we discussed. Nick was a sergeant when JJD was hired. Nick only worked with JJD under him for about four months of the time JJD was in Auburn. He stated that DeAngelo was not a very good cop because he did not go very deep. He stopped people sometimes. Nick Willick stated that he knew JJD to be a passive person.

Mr. Willick also states that JJD did not like to be corrected or to be told how to do anything a different way or to be told how to do something better. Also while on calls he frequently if not always invaded peoples space where he would stand too close for comfort. He would put his hand on you and appear to be overly nice. There had been complaints that JJD was rude and that his attitude was not the best on a call. Mr. Willick said as well that JJD was never late. He was not overweight but seemed to sort of waddle when he walked. He was always eating cookies and chips so they called him junk food Joey. Even so JJD was athletic. JJD also had a moustache when he was working there which is something all of the sleuths on this case already have heard as well as seen in photographs taken during that time frame.

I finally got to ask and receive an answer to my question which was did JJD have a stutter? Mr. Willick said JJD did not stutter although he had a high pitched voice when he was excited.

There were about 17-18 officers in Auburn at the time JJD worked there. According to Willick JJD filed a workmen's compensation claim against Auburn and part of what he had to do was speak to a counselor. JJD apparently stated that Willick never liked him and Willick stressed him out. This was after the firing of JJD for shoplifting.

When I asked Mr. Willcik about the report of someone prowling at his home after JJD was fired he says that there was a substantial amount of time between the firing and the prowling. JJD apparently admitted to the prowling to his workman's compensation counselor and that is when he stated Willick never liked him. Because there was a substantial bit of time between the firing and the prowling no connection was made between JJD and the prowler. He has also said that the arrest of a former cop gives law enforcement a black eye. Mr. Willick did not connect JJD with it initially as they had just moved into a new house on a cul-de-sac and there were no curtains put up yet.

They had only put screens in a day or two before the prowling and Willick did state there were footprints outside the home as he went to investigate after his daughter had seen someone outside.

Willick stated that when JJD was arrested for shoplifting and prosecuted he was going to appeal the conclusion.

In articles I have read since the arrest, retired police chief Nick Willick has said he is embarrassed to have worked with DeAngelo. He has also said that this reflects not only his department but the arrest of a former cop gives Law Enforcement a black eye.

## CHAPTER FOUR

## Crimes in East Sacramento & South Sacramento

## 1976-1979

East Area Rapist attacks begin Rancho Cordova, California

June 18, 1976     Rancho Cordova

July 17, 1976     Carmichael

August 29, 1976 Rancho Cordova

September 4/5 1976 Rancho Cordova

October 5, 1976 Citrus Heights

October 9, 1976 Rancho Cordova

October 18, 1976 – two rapes one in Carmichael one in Rancho Cordova on the same night

November 10, 1976 Citrus Heights

December 18, 1976 Fair Oaks

There were 20 attacks in 1977 in and around Sacramento. One of the attacks was again November 10, 1977 DeAngelo's wedding anniversary.

There were 14 attacks in 1978. Only two appear to have been in the Sacramento area while the other attacks were in Stockton, Modesto, Davis, Concord, San Ramon, San Jose and Danville, California.

In 1979 there were 7 attacks – only one in Rancho Cordova, California while the other six occurred in Walnut Creek, Danville, Fremont and then Goleta. All of the attacks were rapes and assaults. Obviously the EAR suspect had become more mobile. What was going on in his life that he began to travel outside his known hunting grounds? As it turned out DeAngelo moved to Southern California for a while. Not far from his relatives in the area and not far from Manuela Witthuhn a murder victim in 1981 and eventually Janelle Cruz who was murdered in 1986 less than 2 miles away from the crime scene of Manuela in Irvine, CA.

When the Visalia Ransacker moved to Auburn as we now know and began his attacks of rape and terror in Sacramento the Sheriff's Department and news media did not tell the public of the rapes that seemed to begin in June 1976. From June until October the public was unaware and lacked any warning or tools with which to protect themselves. There were four months plus in the beginning that the public might have been able to help find this man as he was in the beginning of his serial rape series. Law Enforcement had to make a judgment call about whether to inform the public and risk warning EAR they were looking for him or whether to wait in making a public announcement about the perp hoping they would catch him in the beginning. We know when a perpetrator is just beginning a series that is when they make the most mistakes. EAR was just getting warmed up.

In the beginning as the public slowly began to be aware of this perpetrator and begin to be able to define his M.O. the reports of prowling's among neighbors and friends were terrifying. This criminal was not your run of the mill rapist or prowler, or peeper. He had an edge, a defiance about him from the start. It was noticed from the beginning if one was paying attention that he was a real threat. An instinct told all who encountered him that he could and was capable of killing. The victims of this man knew that he walked on the edge. JJD knew exactly what he was doing to his victims psychologically. His threat was not just to their bodies or their safety, his threat went far deeper because of the fear. The energy he created was the very real idea that came through loud and clear. If you move, I will kill you.

JJD said these words in many varying ways, but the intent and the threat were real. And, we knew it. He meant it. This was the most terrifying about the psychological game this madman played. He really was not only about power and control, this criminal, this creep knew how to gain power and how to manipulate it and how to keep it. JJD became a master at running not only the public and using our fears against us, he became a master at running the police departments in each jurisdiction around in circles.

It did not help that in the 1970's that there were other serial rapists in their towns, it did not help that rape was something that a lot of officers did not really want on their call list for the night. It did not help that there were so many sightings or even imagined sightings of this creep. The detectives and officers likely were weary not long after this man ran amok in Sacramento. They did the best they could with the tools available at the time. They were in the middle of switching from days gone by and protocols that were outdated to trying to get up to speed with the new technology staring them in the face... computers. The switchover from the dark ages into improving everything they did, improving how everything was done was a sign of the times. In every jurisdiction. I understand, I was there and installed computers for a living. The resistance to change was real. It took time to improve procedure and implement new programs. Even having a female officer and then female detectives was brand new really. Thank goodness for the victims in the rape cases committed by EAR that at the time they had a sensitive, empathetic Detective by the name of Carol Daly in Sacramento. At least she counseled approximately 27 of the rape victims in Sacramento alone. Carol made sure the victims were heard, that they were supported and referred to all those who could try to help them.

In the beginning we were dealing with an unpredictable man who would do anything to stay free and to make sure that his self-preservation came first.

Sometime in the beginning in Sacramento there was a report of neighbors who called in a prowler or a something suspicious going on at the neighbors. Wanting someone to come and investigate the call came in. This call was near Dolcetto and Dawes in Rancho Cordova which is and was a small outlying area in the east area of Sacramento, California. The people who called the report in had been asked to watch over their neighbors home while they were out of town. Apparently the couple had heard suspicious noises coming from what should have been an empty home nearby. They should not have been hearing anything coming from the home or from the backyard, but they did. A couple of officers went through the backyard looking for anyone or anything strange. Nothing seemed out of place or unusual. While discussing the noises with the couple who had called in the reports and in checking the exterior of the house everything seemed normal. The officers left the scene.

Within a few minutes of the officers' departure the couple again called police saying the prowler was still there. When an officer pulled up where once the garage door had been shut it now hung wide open. The neighbors heard a couple of bumps and thumps and when looking out from their home saw a white male about 5' 9" tall, with blonde hair maybe 16-18 years old jump from the roof. He was wearing military fatigues; he ran straight to the back fence jumping over easily. When the officer peered over the back fence after the suspect he noted a lined cement canal void of water. Not far away as one could run down this creek bed there was a school and school yard. The perpetrator was long gone so the Detective returned to the home. "As he was returning to the open garage door he saw a piece of firewood about 18 inches long. It was covered in blood. A lot of thick blood."

Investigating further the officer then decided to check the interior of the home. The officer in this case was Detective Richard Shelby. He states that as he began to enter the home he could feel the presence of death. Everything inside seemed fine as he entered. Something definitely felt off so he had his handgun ready. Going from room to room looking for a source of blood. Continuing his search room to room mostly in the dark, but carrying a small flashlight Detective Shelby continued through each room.. Nothing appeared out of place and was very neat. He says "That is, right up until I peered at the floor between a night stand and the headboard. There, with its head partially under the bed, lay the family dog. It lay right where it had sought escape from evil. That pup had been struck so hard it was disemboweled." He states "Apparently I had located the source of blood on that piece of firewood."

In this story, and in various reports, in the books like Richard Shelby's and Larry Crompton's, the stories of each attack are all horrific and terrible. The one that Detective Shelby experienced in this particular story shows all at once just how cruel and evil a man committed all of these crimes.

In the beginning what was known was this very accurate report which came in over and over and over: In his book Sudden Terror, Larry Crompton writes "The rapist tied them, blindfolded them, gagged them, and put guns to their heads; they listened while he cocked the weapon and they waited for that final pain they knew would soon follow. He put knives to their throats, drawing blood from the passive, and he smashed his fists and clubs into the faces of those who resisted. He shot and clubbed to death those who kept resisting and then he clubbed to death those who didn't resist." "He terrorized, always he terrorized."

February 17, 1977 **ARTICLE**

A prowler shot and seriously wounded a 15-year-old youth who was chasing him in a residential neighborhood in east Sacramento at 10:30 o'clock last night.

Rodney Richard (Blank) who lives on Ripon Court was in critical condition when he was admitted to Sutter Memorial Hospital. He was shot in the abdomen.

A hospital aide today advised Detective Jay Pane that the youth emerged from surgery in a stable and alert condition.

The prowler, described only as male, white and long haired, escaped despite a police cordon on the neighborhood.

The neighborhood is near the Glenbrook District. Detectives are considering the possibility the prowler might have been the east area rapist who has sexually assaulted 15 women in 16 months including one last Jan. 19 in the Glenbrook area.

The youth's father, Raymond told investigators his son just had entered the house from the garage when they heard a noise in the back yard. Miller said he and Rodney went into the yard and saw the figure of a man in shadows. The father said the man ran, and he and his son chased him across the street. **END OF ARTICLE**

The CREEP Among Us * Anne Penn

## Lurker Shoots Youth

A prowler shot and seriously wounded an 18-year-old youth who was chasing him in a residential neighborhood in east Sacramento at 10:30 o'clock last night.

Rodney Richard ▆▆▆▆, who lives on Ripon Court, was in critical condition when he was admitted to Sutter Memorial Hospital. He was shot in the abdomen.

A hospital aide today advised Detective Jay Pane that the youth emerged from surgery in a stable and alert condition.

The prowler, described only as male, white and long-haired, escaped despite a police cordon on the neighborhood.

The neighborhood is near the Glenbrook District. Detectives are considering the possibility the prowler might have been the east area rapist who has sexually assaulted 15 women in 16 months, including one last Jan. 19 in the Glenbrook area.

The youth's father, Raymond, told investigators his son just had entered the house from the garage when they heard a noise in the back yard. Miller said he and Rodney went into the yard and saw the figure of a man in shadows.

The father said the man ran, and he and his son chased him across the street.

The CREEP Among Us * Anne Penn

## East Area Rapist Attacks Girl, 13

The East Area rapist broke into a Sacramento condominium early today, raping a 13-year-old girl after he awakened and tied up her mother.

The 27th attack in 17 months occurred on La Riviera Drive near Watt Avenue in the College Greens section of the city about 3 a.m., said sheriff's Chief Deputy Fred Reese.

The rapist spent about two hours in the home, raping the girl, then fondling her as she sat tied in a chair.

He entered the condominium by forcing open a sliding glass door, Reese said.

Once inside, the rapist awakened the mother, tied her in her bed, placed china on her back and said if he heard the dishes rattle, he would cut off the daughter's fingers, police said. The rapist then led the 13-year-old into another room and attacked her.

After the ski-masked, armed man left the home, the girl and the woman screamed until neighbors heard them. A neighbor then followed the screams into the home and untied the two victims. She was the youngest victim in the terrifying series of attacks, police said. In his last 10 rapes, he has victimized sleeping couples in cases where he has tied the men in bed, then led the women to other parts of the homes for sexual assaults.

The East Area rapist last struck Oct. 29 north of Whitney Avenue.

After this morning's attack was reported about 5 a.m., sheriff's deputies took into custody a possible suspect in an El Camino Avenue restaurant. The man was questioned, taken to the scene of the rape and held in custody about two hours before he was released.

City police simultaneously—
See Back Page, A26, Col. 5

# Rapist *Continued From Page A1* 11/6/77

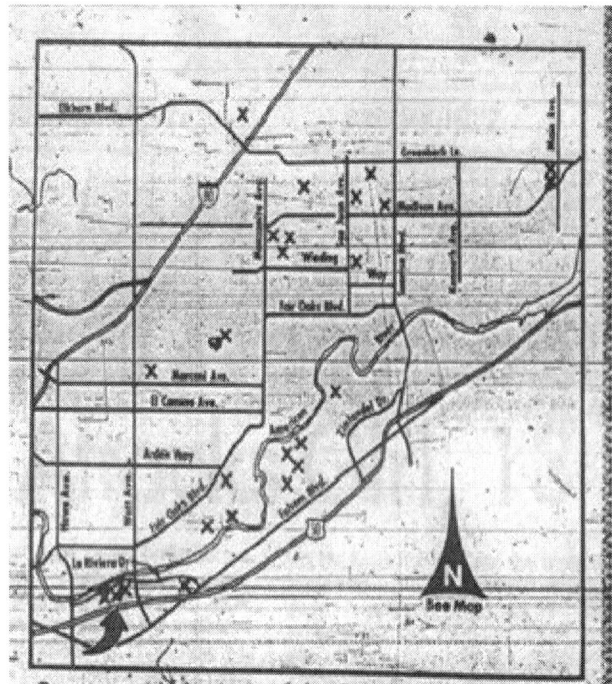

*Crosses mark the sites of the East Area rapist's attacks.*

broadcast a description of a suspicious car that had been spotted in the area at the time of the rape. The car was described as a 1966 blue Chevrolet with Arizona license plates.

The rapist has struck 25 times in the East and North Areas of Sacramento County, once in the South Area and once in Stockton since his first rape was reported June 18, 1976.

He has been the subject of the most intensive manhunt in the county's history, police have said. Detectives have checked out in one fashion or another more than 5,000 men reported as possible suspects. Still, they have no idea of whom they are looking for or what kind of man he really is, detectives say.

The rapist was described in the spring as a man in a "homosexual panic" caused by feelings of sexual inadequacy attributed to his having a small penis. After talking to several more victims, however, sheriff's deputies Tuesday revised the sexual description of the rapist to say he has an average size penis; neither abnormally small nor large.

His strikes are punctuated by silence in what sheriff's Detective Carol Daly has described as "mental torture on the victims, not just physical attacks."

"His big thing is being master over their minds once he gets them tied up," she said. "That's his big trip."

## The CREEP Among Us * Anne Penn

November 1977 - The East Area Rapist broke into a Sacramento Condominium early today, raping a 13-year-old girl after he awakened and tied up her mother. The 27$^{th}$ attack in 17 months occurred on La Riviera Drive near Watt Avenue in the College Greens section of the city about 3:00 a.m. said Sheriffs Chief Deputy Fred Reese.

The rapist spent about two hours in the home, raping the girl, then fondling her as she sat tied in a chair. He entered the condominium by forcing open a sliding glass door Reese said.

Once inside, the rapist awakened the mother, tied her in her bed, placed china on her back and said if he heard the dishes rattle, he would cut off the daughter's fingers, police said. The rapist then led the 13-year-old into another room and attacked her.

After the ski masked, armed man left the home, the girl and the woman screamed until neighbors heard them. A neighbor then followed the screams into the home and untied the two victims. She was the youngest victim in the terrifying series of attacks, police said. In his last 10 rapes, he has victimized sleeping couples in cases where he has tied the men in bed, then led the women to other parts of the home for sexual assaults.

The East Area Rapist last struck October 29 north of Whitney Avenue. After this morning's attack was reported at 5:00 a.m. sheriff's deputies took into custody a possible suspect in an El Camino Avenue restaurant. The man was questioned, taken to the scene of the rape and held in custody about two hours before he was released. City police simultaneously broadcast a description of a suspicious car that had been spotted in the area at the time of the rape. The car was described as a 1966 blue Chevrolet with Arizona license plates.

The rapist has struck 25 times in the East and North Area of Sacramento County, once in the South Area and once in Stockton since his first rape was reported June 18, 1976. He has been the subject of the most intensive manhunt in the County's history police have said.

Detectives have checked out in one fashion or another more than 5000 men reported as possible suspects. Still they have no idea of whom they are looking for or what kind of man he really is, detectives say.

The rapist was described in the spring as a man in a "homosexual panic" caused by feelings of sexual inadequacy attributed to his having a small penis. After talking to several more victims however, sheriff's deputies Tuesday revised the sexual description of the rapist to say he has an average size penis neither abnormally small nor large.

His strikes are punctuated by silence in what sheriff's Detective Carol Daly has described as mental torture on the victims, not just physical attacks. His big thing is being master over their minds once he gets them tied up she said. "That's his big trip." **END OF ARTICLE**

## The CREEP Among Us * Anne Penn

Sacramento Bee article 10-21-77
Warren Holloway & Thom Akeman
The East Area Rapist shifted to the Foothill Farms area today to attack a sleeping couple, Ransack their home and leave them to be untied by their two small children, Sheriff's Deputies reported.

The rapist entered the home northeast of the Elkhorn Boulevard and Diablo Drive intersection about 3 a.m., sheriff's deputies said. He wore a ski mask and carried a pistol and a knife to overpower the couple in their bedroom, deputies said. It was the 25$^{th}$ attack in 16 months attributed to the rapist. Twenty-two have occurred in the north or east area, one in the south area, and one in Stockton. The rapist last struck October 1 when he raped a 17-year-old girl who was visiting her boyfriend in the LaRiviera-Folsom Blvd. area. In today's attack, the rapist forced open a side door on the garage, then broke through a kitchen door to enter the home. This is one of the few forced entries of the East Area Rapist. The man has routinely entered the homes of his victims by snapping open sliding glass doors. Neither of the doors in today's entry were secured with deadbolts.

The rapist awakened the sleeping couple, tied the man on the bed, then led the woman to another part of the house where he tied her and repeatedly raped her, deputies said. It is the same pattern the rapist had followed in his last nine strikes.

"As sure as we can be, this was the East Area Rapist. He had the same M.O. Sure the attacker was gone, they awakened their children and had them untie them." They called the sheriff's office at 4:35 a.m. The spokesman refused to reveal further details of the rapist's activities in the home or to say if the attacker left any messages for the police or press, as he has done in other strikes.

The rapist first struck June 18, 1976. His first 16 attacks were against women who were either home alone or with their small children. The invader awakened and tied up the children in at least one case.

The last nine attacks attributed to the East Area Rapist have involved couples. His pattern is to awaken them as they are in their bedrooms, point the gun and knife at them, order the woman to tie the man, place dishes on the man, and tell him his wife will be killed if the dishes rattle, lead the woman into another part of the house, rape her, tie her in a chair, ransack the house, then return to rape the woman again.

Only two of the rapist's attacks have started outside the victim's homes, with one woman and one couple confronted at gunpoint in front of their homes. The other 23 have occurred after the rapist broke into the homes of his sleeping victims.

## The CREEP Among Us * Anne Penn

The rapist has been described as a "paranoid schizophrenic" acting in a homosexual panic caused by feelings of sexual inadequacy.

That was contained in a psychological profile released by the sheriff's detectives in May.

The terrorist has attacked irregularly since then, striking in the south area May 28, in Stockton September 6, back in the east area October 1, and in the north area today.
END OF ARTICLE

Of note from this article is the date of attack after a break during the summer. September 5, 1977 was labor day. The day after that there is an attack in Stockton. Each time EAR skipped summer he would attack as soon as possible after the labor day weekend. In 1976 Labor day was September 6. An attack that year was right before the labor day holiday and he attacked two days in a row. September 4$^{th}$ and 5$^{th}$ that year which was 1978. The Visalia Ransacker break-ins also occurred around the Labor day weekend. Prowlings were reported. September 3, 1973. Prowlings were also reported in September of 1975. September 11, 1975 there was the attemped abduction of Beth Snelling and the murder of her father Claude Snelling in Visalia. There were attacks during the summer, but not as much as other times of the year.

During the East Area Rapist series I have only listed a few of the crimes perpetrated in Sacramento. If there was a break in his crime sprees in Sacramento during 1976 – 1979 it was only because EAR was attacking in other places and in other jurisdictions. He attacked in all of the following communities and when he moved to the Southern California areas to begin committing murders in earnest he became known as The Original Night Stalker. The attacks by EAR by area are listed: Stockton, Modesto, Davis, Concord, San Ramon, San Jose, Fremont, Walnut Creek, Goleta. As Law Enforcement connects the dots investigating other crimes in California and elsewhere there may be other monikers to be added to the list in every book written about this guy.

The CREEP Among Us * Anne Penn

Morrison Creek West South Sacramento my childhood home was on the right side beyond the homes that butted up against the creek path behind their homes. It was 53$^{rd}$ Avenue. To the left side is Parkway

Previous page photograph: This is where supposedly EAR jumped over fences and fell into the canal and as the story went he went to a hospital with a shoulder injury the day after the attack on Fourth Parkway, but left prior to being helped. I never bought that story because EAR had plenty of time to just walk away and he also knew the neighborhood and creek system well. No one was chasing him he did not need to hurry. He just walked away after the Fourth Parkway attack in my opinion.

Canals run throughout Sacramento behind houses, throughout neighborhoods East and South. The fact that Sacramento is a River town with levees, and multiple water sources made it so these canals were and are everywhere to make sure that when it rains in Sacramento there is somewhere for the water to go to avoid flooding. EAR preferred this way of travel and as it turned out he travelled this way all over the State.

## Chapter Five

## Possible Connections to other crimes

.... Since we are fairly certain about EAR's travels down Hwy 99 to his attacks in Stockton, Modesto, Fresno and possibly other places I have to suspect it is possible that Kathleen Neff could be an EAR victim. By 1980 people were calling him the Original Night Stalker down in Southern California because murders were occurring there. The Offerman and Manning murders were in December 1979. Next was my uncle Lyman Smith and his wife Charlene March 13, 1980. That summer in August 1980 the Harrington's from Laguna Niguel or Dana Point were also murdered. Then there is a gap until 1981. In 1980 the DeAngelo's purchased the house where 38 years later we would find him.

On October 16, 1980 Kathleen Neff became a victim of murder. She was in South Sacramento to drop her car off for repair on Florin Road. If you recall the street name, and if you have read extensively on these cases you will recall that there was an abduction attempt of a 17-year-old female in February 1978 on Florin Road near Florin Shopping Mall. In articles this was actually described as a robbery attempt. I would bet it was an abduction attempt. A very fast car chase ensued by a highway patrol officer as he tried to capture the suspect. The officer did his best while giving chase, but ended up being injured while the perpetrator got away. This abduction attempt happened not long after the

Maggiore murder February 2, 1978 in Rancho Cordova.

Kathleen Neff was abducted from the car shop area on Florin Road October 16, 1980. The photograph of Ms. Neff is on the next pages along with the police description of what occurred on that date in 1980. The report tells where they found her body. Twenty-three days after Ms. Neff dropped off her car on Florin Road her body was found off Elliot Ranch Road which is a 27-minute drive from Florin Road as one travels south and can be gotten to on a parallel road called Franklin Blvd. which is not far from Highway 99. This crime has never been solved.

Back in 1980 the area where her body was discovered by pheasant hunters was still very rural. We know that EAR was familiar with Florin Road and the areas off Florin Road as he attacked on 4th Parkway which was a stone's throw away from Florin Road as well as the Florin Mall. We know that EAR was familiar with escape routes and creeks also in that area. EAR had much familiarity of the areas off Seamas and Casilada as well as having knowledge of how to travel south on Hwy 99, frontage roads, and the Sacramento River Levee. Because we know of this familiarity I have to think the Sacramento County Sheriff's Department is looking at Ms. Neff's murder for Joseph J. DeAngelo. In October 1980 where was Mr. DeAngelo? He had purchased a home in Citrus Heights. Was he back from areas in Southern California temporarily? Ms. Neff's body happened to be discovered November 8, 1980 – ironically on JJD's 35th birthday. The majority of JJD attacks over time were shown to have happened in the month of October.

**This was taken from the Sacramento County Sheriff's website about unsolved murders.**
**Victim:**Kathleen E. Neff
**Location:**Elliot Ranch Road
**Date of Occurrence:**November 8, 1980

**Synopsis:**
On the morning of October 16, 1980 Kathy Neff, a 21 year old female, dropped off her vehicle at a vehicle dealership on Florin Road for service, with plans to pick up the vehicle later that same day. The next day, when family and friends could not locate Kathy, a missing person's report was filed. On November 8, 1980, some pheasant hunters in the area of Elliot Ranch Road, discovered Kathy's remains.

**It would be good to know who murdered Ms. Neff all those years ago. This map shows how quick and easy it would have been to abduct Ms. Neff and dump her body not far from Florin road using frontage roads.

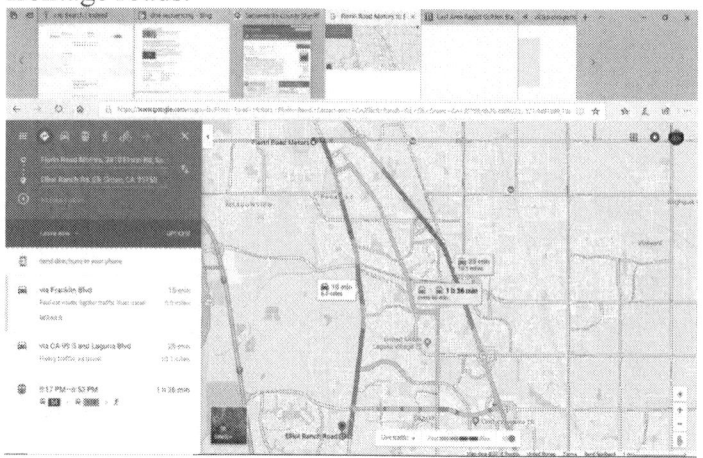

I reported this to Sac Sheriff's recently: The date of the discovery of Ms. Neff's body corresponds to the birthday of your suspect Joseph James DeAngelo. His attacks frequently were in October each year with October being the month he was most active throughout the series. DeAngelo is known to pay attention to anniversaries and timelines that are meaningful to him. Mr. DeAngelo also lived in the area at the time of this abduction. He was also known to drag a victim or try to abduct victims. There was another known abduction attempt on Florin Road in February 1978 where a Highway Patrol Officer gave chase and was injured. Mr. DeAngelo changed his MO several times over the course of his crimes and from place to place. He was extremely familiar with the area of attack and also the area the victim's body was found. If I were you I would be checking every piece of physical evidence for DeAngelo's DNA. END OF MY TIP

I am certain Law Enforcement is working very hard and are crossing all of their T's and dotting all of their I's. I am certain they have looked at this crime and will either eliminate him as a suspect here or we will hear about the outcome later on.

Or... it is possible that the crime spree which began in Sacramento from 1978-1980 and was the work of Charlene and Gerald Gallego could have killed Ms. Neff? The Gallegos were not apprehended until November 17, 1980. Ms. Neff disappeared in October 1980. Sacramento County Sheriff's office had their hands full in the latter half of the 1970's into 1980. I suppose it is no wonder if they would have been relieved when the East Area Rapist appeared to vanish from their area. April 1978 was the last date of attack most noted by people who write about JJD's crimes in Sacramento. In reality JJD attacked one more time that we know of in Rancho Cordova in 1979. And then he was supposedly gone from Sacramento. At least for all intents and purposes as reports have shown.

Also what I and others think at this point is that JJD was laying low. He essentially was quiet in Sacramento where he had begun living full time from about 1980 on. Any crimes that occurred after 1979 in Sacramento were not attributed to him any longer. It seems that everyone there including the Sacramento Law Enforcement Investigator's thought EAR had moved on. Prowling's, peeping's, breaking into homes were less concentrated and EAR was no longer in the forefront of anyone's mind. We all breathed a sigh of relief. This was intentional and designed by JJD in order for him to not be noticed in the place where he lived. For years' people have speculated if he had left as in moved to another state, died, or been imprisoned. I never believed he was dead. I wish I had been able to convince myself that he was. I knew in my gut that he was there.

The East Area Rapist moved very quickly to a back burner in the minds of the authorities and the public when beginning in September 1978 the Gallegos couple began a series of abductions and murders. In the two years they were operating in and around Sacramento they murdered 10 women in California, Oregon and Nevada. Abductions were many times orchestrated by Charlene so her husband could carry out his gruesome crimes. Gerald abducted a bartender coming off shift in West Sacramento. He abducted two girls from the Country Club Mall near Arden Way. The bodies were typically driven up Highway 80 towards Auburn which is a very beautiful area. Off the highway he would walk the victim out into the woods killing them at the site where later their bodies would be found.

The one loan rape committed by The East Area Rapist that followed in March 1979 in Rancho Cordova was most likely just a blip as Sacramento was searching for a known serial killer in their own territory. What is interesting about this timeline and these two very evil men who operated simultaneously for a moment is this: When JJD, AKA The East Area Rapist was still working as a police officer in Auburn, CA the Gallegos couple were dumping bodies right off Highway 80 in the foothills not far from Auburn. They did this during the fall of 1978 and into 1979. Gerald was arrested November 17, 1980. A relative calm followed at last for the most part and was felt by all Sacramentans as EAR had left according to rumor, and the Gallegos couple had been stopped. As we know JJD was still in Sacramento that year as noted by the purchase of the home on Canyon Oak. We also know that EAR had moved on and beginning in the fall of 1979 had become the serial killer he had promised to become attacking in Southern California and hoping Law Enforcement would not recognize that it was him. One failed attack in October 1979 in Danville was followed by the brutal murders of Dr. Robert Offerman and Dr. Debra Manning December 30, 1979 in Goleta.

In addition to EAR feeling the heat from his own attacks in Sacramento he had to know about this serial killer who was dumping bodies in his own backyard. He also had to know how extensive the manhunt was for Gerald Gallego. Sacramento was really working the Gallego case. I recall it vividly as well because EAR had us in his grip from 1976-1978. The news then began to tell us of young women who vanished in and around the same territories. Of course we had no idea then that an Auburn Police Officer named Joseph DeAngelo was right up the road. DeAngelo was driving the backroads from Auburn to Citrus Heights and East Sacramento committing his rapes in 1976, 1977, 1978 and 1979. The news became about this new series of crimes. Murder trumps rape and did in these cases. Gallegos first killed in September 1978 that we know of. By then the attacks in Sacramento by EAR seemed to stop as of April of the same year. EAR went on to attack some more in Stockton, Danville, San Jose, Walnut Creek, Modesto, San Ramon, Concord and Fremont. He did not return to the Sacramento area to rape until March 1979. Then as we know from all of the extensive media reports in July 1979 JJD was arrested in Sacramento County for shoplifting and fired from the Auburn Police Department. I think it is a very plausible theory to conclude that not only was EAR feeling Sacramento closing in based on the Maggiore murders that occurred in February 1978, but also because a more realistic composite had come out also in the spring of 1978. Add to that the serial killer who showed up intensifying a manhunt to stop the Gallego couple whom they had yet to identify, I think it is very possible EAR stayed out of his known hunting grounds because of the intensified police scrutiny as they stepped up activity to find Gerald and Charlene Gallegos.

Here is information about the Gallego couple taken from Wikipedia.

"Gerald Armond Gallego (a.k.a. "Stephen Feil" or "Stephen Styles") was born on 17 July 1946 in Sacramento, California. His mother was a prostitute, while his estranged father was a criminal who in 1955 became the first man executed in the Mississippi gas chamber, for the killing of a police officer during a prison escape. Gallego began his criminal career at age thirteen, when he sexually abused a six-year-old girl. He had 23 arrests and served time after being convicted of robbery prior to his murder spree."

"Gallego worked as a bartender and truck driver. He was married a total of seven times, including two marriages to the same woman. He was still married to a previous wife when he married Charlene Williams."

**"Charlene Adell (Williams) Gallego**

Charlene Adell Williams was born on 10 October 1956 in Stockton, California. She was a smart, shy child from a supportive home. The trajectory of her life began to change when, as a young adult, she started using drugs and alcohol. She had two failed marriages before meeting Galego."

Victims

**Rhonda Scheffler and Kippi Vaught**

On 11 September 1978, two teenagers – Rhonda Scheffler and Kippi Vaught – disappeared from a mall in Sacramento. Charlene lured them to a nearby van, leading to their abduction by the couple. Gerald used a handgun to threaten the girls and tied them up. They drove to Baxter, where Gerald raped and then executed the girls, each with a single shot to the back of their heads.

**My comments**: This was the Country Club Mall near Arden Way in Sacramento not far from the American River and the Sacramento River which was not far from EAR and his hunting grounds Baxter if right off Highway 80 on the way to Auburn.

**Brenda Judd and Sandra Colley**

On 24 June 1979, Brenda Judd and Sandra Colley were abducted from the Washoe County Fair in Reno, Nevada. Charlene later testified that Gerald beat the girls to death with a shovel or hammer.

Their remains were not found and identified until twenty years later.

There are many unsolved murders, abductions and attacks in and around Sacramento, Auburn and other counties as we see if they can be connected to JJD moving forward.

## Stacy Ann Redican and Karen Chipman-Twiggs

Similarly, on 24 April 1980, Stacy Ann Redican and Karen Chipman-Twiggs went missing from a Sacramento mall. They were found in July, sexually abused and bludgeoned to death.

## Linda Teresa Aguilar

While hitchhiking on 6 June 1980, Linda Teresa Aguilar – who was pregnant – was abducted, murdered with a blunt object, and buried in a shallow grave.

My comments: This crime happened in the State of Oregon

## Virginia Mochel

On July 17, 1980, 34-year-old Virginia Mochel was abducted from the parking lot of a West Sacramento tavern, where she worked as a bartender. Her skeletal remains, still bound with nylon fishing line, were found three months later outside of Clarksburg. Loops of cord from the victim's neck were admitted as proof of death by strangulation.

## Craig Miller and Mary Elizabeth Sowers

While leaving a fraternity party on 1 November 1980, Craig Miller and Mary Elizabeth Sowers were forced into the Gallego's car at gunpoint. Miller was ordered out of the car and shot; his body was found near Bass Lake, California. The couple returned to their apartment with Sowers, where Gerald sexually abused her before taking her to a field in Placer County, California, where he then executed her."END OF WIKIPEDIA INFORMATION

The CREEP Among Us * Anne Penn

**My comments**: This occurred off Highway 50 in Placer County. Only a 20 to 30-minute drive away from Folsom CA and not far from EAR hunting grounds

Wikipedia states there were ten victims. There were actually eleven. Linda Teresa Aguilar was pregnant. When Gerald saw her and offered her a ride one of the things that motivated him to pick her up was the fact that she was very pregnant. To him that did not matter. He took her life and that of her unborn baby. The count should say eleven perished at the hands of Gerald and Charlene Gallego.

I felt these crimes were important to note as I do think the two criminals had an impact on one another as they were both aware of the news coverage of one another and EAR truly did not want the attention being brought to the area to impact him or stop him in what he had planned, especially after he was fired in the summer of 1979.

There were many serial rapists, and murderers operating in the late 70's. The attention truly was taken away from The East Area Rapist series.

I have included maps of the Sacramento area Highway system to help make clear how Sacramento was actually the hub of where the intersections and highways fed into one another. It was very easy for JJD and the Gallegos to get around.

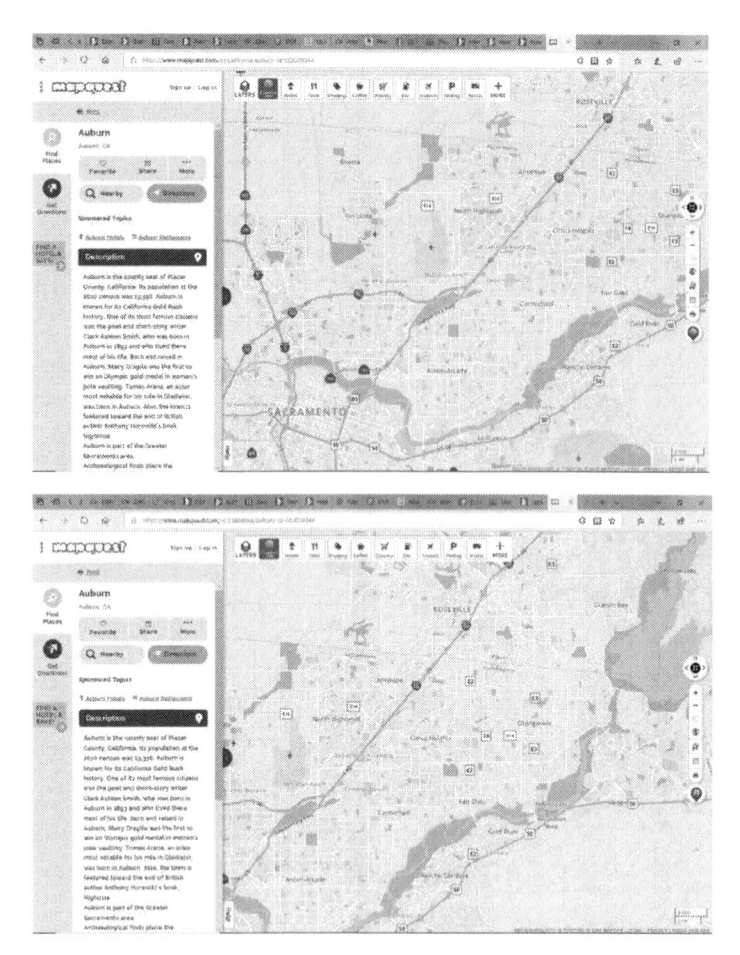

This map shows Highway 80 and Highway 50. On the left side of highway 50 are the attack areas.

To the left side of map is highway 80 which if one travels north you will end up in Auburn

In 20 minutes or less

The CREEP Among Us * Anne Penn

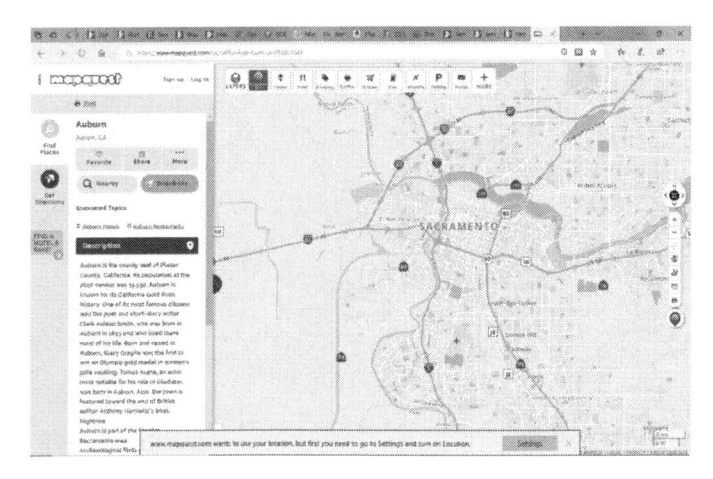

This map shows just how easy it is from Sacramento to hop on any interchange on several highways

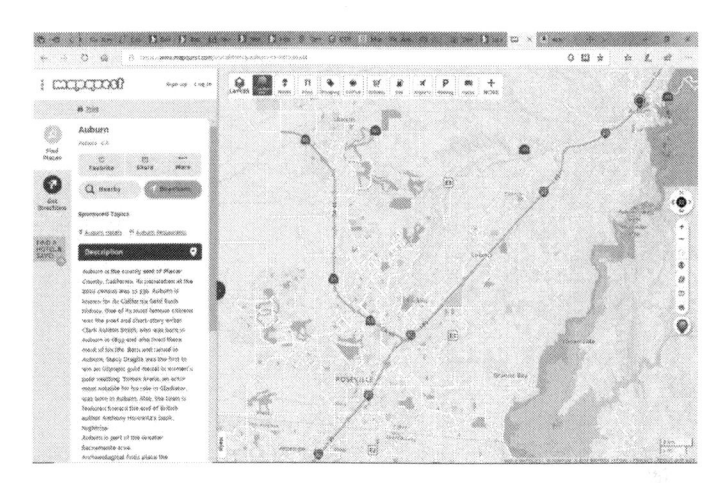

This map shows Highway 80 from Roseville to Auburn bottom of map is Antelope, then Roseville, Loomis, Penryn, and Auburn

## OTHER POSSIBLE CRIMES - POSSIBLE CONNECTIONS

"The unsolved murder of 34-year-old Patricia Neufeld, a young Garden Grove mother, who lived just six blocks from the brother of the DeAngelo is getting a fresh look -- 40 years after it happened.

A group of UC Irvine law students and the pro bono group Innocence Rights of Orange County, are starting to dig into whether Neufeld could be another victim of the accused serial murderer and rapist.

"The similarities between the Golden State Killer's M.O. and what was found at the scene of the crime for Patricia Neufeld, are strikingly similar," Della Donna, Innocence Rights, explained.

The lawyers say they found out Neufeld was bludgeoned to death with a bowling pin that was left behind. The infants who were with her were unharmed. The house wasn't ransacked -- the brutal killing was two days before Thanksgiving back in 1978.

"We have reason to believe that a lot of golden state killer cases were based upon opportunity. He would be familiar with the neighborhood, he would start stalking people and neighbors. And we believe he came to his brother's house shortly before the holiday and committed this murder," Donna explained. Another case, the killing of Fountain Valley's Joan

Anderson could also be linked to the East Area Rapist.

The same group of lawyers brought this to the attention of the Orange County District Attorney's Office, which is now investigating." END OF ARTICLE

So now that there has been an arrest there are many or maybe most who believe we will discover that this criminal killed others who had yet to be connected to the man with the monikers EAR, (East Area Rapist) ONS, (Original Night Stalker) and GSK, (Golden State Killer). Now known as JJD.

I have tried to piece together this puzzle for years. Many others also have tried to put this puzzle together. I no longer wanted this story to define my fear. I now know after the five months plus that JJD has been in jail that I may never totally get over a lifetime of nervousness at dark or being cautious when hiking or walking with the idea in mind that I am safe alone. I did grow up in the town this man decided to terrorize. I lived in Sacramento in many of the areas he struck. In my original books I had stated I thought I was close by as this man grew from a boy into a young man. I was wrong about his age. Now we know he was not so young when the attacks began in Visalia.

I was close by in 1976-1978 while he broke in and terrorized many young women and then couples. I was lucky to have been missed along the way but shudder to think about the closeness to my geographic locations he would strike. I know there are many women that were in Sacramento who feel the same way. I know Sacramento well and I have been to all of the areas he struck. The descriptions given of neighborhoods in Sacramento I have been to having lived, worked, and played there. In 1978 one minute away from where EAR attacked off Seamas & Piedmont an incident happened in the building I resided in. I had told of the mysterious break-in where someone went through my underwear drawers and also the drawers of the woman who lived upstairs from me. We both had long blonde hair at the time. We never figured out what had happened as nothing else was disturbed in either residence. A few weeks later EAR attacked just down the street. What are the odds that this killer not only came from where I did, but then eventually would kill people who were members of our family?

In March 1980 Lyman and Charlene Smith were brutally murdered. They had the right to live out their lives. Lyman should have been allowed to continue bringing up his children, to become a Judge if that was in the cards. Maybe Charlene would have had the children she so desired. Lyman Robert (Bob) had a real life with ambitions and plans. Lyman loved his family and he was loved. My grandfather Lyman Senior loved his son so much. When he was so viciously murdered for no apparent reason; my grandfather was never the same.

There were many other families who lost people they loved and people who were needed. All of the murder victims have been missed since the day this evil came into their lives.

Now that we know where this creep, this man actually came from and in addition finding out what he did for a living while committing crimes we can piece together the actual story of how JJD carried out his crimes. While an active police officer JJD is accused of raping and murdering people in Sacramento and other counties in 1976,77,78 and 1979. He has been charged with murdering the Maggiore's in February 1978 in the Rancho Cordova neighborhood they resided in. Walking their dog that long ago evening turned out to be a very deadly thing to do. To date JJD has been charged with 13 murders which includes Professor Claude Snelling's murder in Visalia in 1975. In the meantime, Law Enforcement will try to connect JJD with unsolved murders in the state of California over the last 42 plus years. While we wait the prosecution and defense are working on the details of what will be one of the biggest cases with the largest number of jurisdictions trying their cases in one huge trial that has ever been done.

Personally I find it satisfies me to know that JJD sits in a jail 2 blocks from the prosecuting attorney's and the District Attorney in Sacramento. That is why the term Just Desserts fits this situation perfectly.

The CREEP Among Us * Anne Penn

May 18, 2018

Sacramento Bee article:

## THE SACRAMENTO BEE

### East Area Rapist arrest has police scouring old files

Cold cases studied to see whether he can be charged in other crimes

The previous article typed for clarity:

When authorities in Sacramento announced the arrest of a suspect in the East Area Rapist case last month, 60-year-old Jim Sigle in Alabama immediately took notice, they finally caught the guy Sigle thought to himself. "It just doesn't seem right that this could happen and there not be somebody held accountable." Like countless others who have lost friends to unsolved cold cases, Sigle was hoping the arrest of Joseph James De Angelo would solve the October 16, 1980, disappearance of his one-time girlfriend, Kathy Emillia Neff.

Neff, 21, vanished after dropping her car off for service at a Mazda dealership on Florin Road; her body was found by pheasant hunters three weeks later at the end of a gravel road near the Valley Hi Country Club. No one was ever arrested in the slaying, and Neff's case remains one of the Sacramento County Sheriff's Department's pending cold case homicides.

Despite DeAngelo's arrest as an alleged serial rapist and killer, sheriff's officials say the circumstances of the Neff killing lead them to believe it is not connected to the East Area Rapist crimes. But the department and other law enforcement agencies across California are taking a fresh look at various cold cases and tips from the public to determine whether there is some previously unseen link to other unsolved crimes.

"Some of those (tips) may have valuable information that on its surface may not seem to be relevant, but there is always that possibility that it's an extra clue," Sheriff's Sgt. Shaun Hampton said.

So far, DeAngelo faces 12* homicide counts from slayings between 1978 and 1986 in Orange, Sacramento, Santa Barbara and Ventura counties, and authorities say they believe he roamed the state committing a string of crimes that may not yet be fully known.

In Tulare County, where the Visalia Ransacker" is suspected of breaking into dozens of homes from April 1974 through December 1975, police have refocused their attention on the unsolved September 11, 1975, homicide.

That case involves the slaying of Claude Snelling, a 45-year-old journalism professor at the College of the Sequoias. Snelling was shot trying to save his 16-year-old daughter, who was in the process of being abducted from their home by a man wearing a ski mask and carrying a gun.

"Obviously, that's still under investigation and we're aware of the DeAngelo arrest," Visalia police Sgt. Damon Maurice said. "We will submit the case to the District Attorney here soon, and it will be up to them if they want to file charges against anybody, including Mr. DeAngelo."

Visalia police spent years trying to solve the case, and always thought it was tied to the Visalia Ransacker," a burglar who would steal odd items or move things around a victim's home, according to a 2017 Fresno Bee story detailing the mystery. The East Area Rapist had similar habits, and authorities said after DeAngelo's arrest that they believe both serial cases are linked.

DeAngelo had a history in the Visalia area, serving as a police officer in Exeter from 1973 until 1976 while the "Ransacker" crimes were being committed in Visalia 11 miles away.

There is no DNA evidence from the Snelling killing like the samples used to arrest DeAngelo, but officials say he still is a suspect. "There are some detectives that will tell you they believe he killed Claude Snelling," said Sacramento County District Attorney Anne Marie Schubert, whose cold-case focus on the East Area Rapist helped lead to the arrest.

Tulare County District Attorney Tim Ward said he is still waiting for a report from Visalia police on the Snelling murder before a decision is made on whether to file charges. He added that the burglaries are beyond the statute of limitations for prosecution, but that those cases also are being reviewed for any possible evidence. "The only active case that's being looked at is the Snelling case," Ward said, adding that he expects to join district attorneys from other affected counties at a meeting in late June in the Los Angeles area.

"Whether or not we decide that charges could be filed in our case, I'll be there in June whether we have a case to discuss or we have a support role," Ward said.

Prosecutors from the four counties where DeAngelo has been charged in the 12 murders met last week in Santa Barbara to begin discussions on how and where to try the cases jointly. Meanwhile, other agencies are still reviewing case files and reports to see if there are more crimes that should be investigated as possibly tied to DeAngelo.

Police in Auburn, where DeAngelo served as an officer from 1976 until he was fired over a shoplifting incident in 1979, have opened ad internal affairs probe to determine whether there are any cold case crimes that might be attributed to him. Other avenues of investigation are not as solid. Law enforcement officials say they've been receiving tips and suggestions from various people, including amateur online groups that were created while the search for and East Area Rapist suspect was still ongoing. One site, which has not been updated with news of the DeAngelo arrest, offers extensive details about the crimes over the years as well as a link reading, "If you are the East Area Rapist click here."

A separate thread on Reddit contains a post asking whether it is appropriate to report a potential suspect who "vaguely" resembles composite drawings of the rapist. Several similar groups have formed on Facebook, offering links to news stories about the case or suggestions about how to find a suspect.

"My feeling is that the original night stalker must be dead, he was so cold and calculating but obviously psychotic I don't think he would have stopped," one post reads. "I believe he was a police officer or someone up to date with police procedure back in those times…"

Despite the fact that authorities sought such tips from the public for years, hoping someone would help them break the case, they now say DeAngelo's arrest stemmed from DNA evidence and their own investigation. The $50,000 reward that was offered in the case, they say, likely will go unpaid. END OF ARTICLE

- *After this article came out JJD was charged with the 13$^{th}$ murder. Claude Snelling as far as we know was JJD's first murder in

September 1975   He has also been charged with Kidnap charges stemming from crimes in Contra Costa County.

## Chapter Six

## My profile statements and predictions

## Connecting the Dots

So what did I say in my previous book in my profile of the suspect and what is turning out to be true?

As we research where the East Area Rapist lived in the year 1977, and I see what I had suspected, that he was in Sacramento on the opposite side of the American River it just makes me feel quiet, reflective, and speechless.

We let him live among us all of those years. Maybe not on purpose, but the fact is that JJD was right there free to drive past all of us. Free to live a free life, happy to thumb his nose at all of us. I have mixed feelings a month plus after his arrest. I still get the feeling in the pit of my stomach like I swallowed something too heavy to sit in in there. I am quietly speechless as a way to keep the anger from rising in my head and in my soul. Because this man stopped raping in such numbers, because the case had gone cold he could continue over the years with impunity. He knew no one was really looking for him anymore. At least not in Sacramento, or Auburn, or Davis, the list is incredibly long when it comes to all the places he had attacked that had ceased to try to find out who he was. For a very long time the cases were essentially cold. Until the last few years.

JJD was very comfortable, and in the beginning of his quietness in Sacramento he began to stop looking over his shoulder. The older he got in his freedom, the older he looked as he lost his hair, and the young composites looked nothing like him anymore he ceased to ever give a thought to what the cold bars of a cage would feel like on the inside.

I knew he was arrogant. One only has to read through his attacks from start to finish that we are aware of to see and to feel his arrogance and his fury. His rages taken out on all of us probably focused now on those closest to him. His neighbors did not like him. They could feel something was off. He threatened to kill a neighbor's dog. He ended up in the house on Canyon Oak alone for a time. He had a daughter who came to live with him and brought a child of her own.

As I have been investigating this case along with everyone else who cares so much about the details of the last forty-two years initially I thought JJD stayed in Sacramento and the surrounding areas because it was his home turf, and because he was arrogant. After looking into this further I find I believe there was another reason he stayed. He stayed all this time and apparently did not have a plan B for easy escape because besides believing no one would come for him and no one would figure out who he was in time (prior to his death from old age), I believe he stayed because Bonnie was still there. She married and raised a family not far from JJD. It was possible he was watching her from afar for all of those years. Over time it is possible that she would not have recognized the man she had briefly been engaged to all those years ago.

As we connect the dots and see where JJD lived, worked, and wandered in his old hunting grounds I am extremely disturbed at what happened in these cases so that a man was allowed to be free all of these years, mocking the criminal justice system, mocking the victims who were forced to share space in a store, on a road next to him in a car, breathing the same air on a hot summers day. Think about the mere fact that this man who after killing Janelle Cruz in 1986 spent the next thirty-two years doing as he pleased. Going to work, going to the store, mowing his lawn, helping his daughter work on her car, and pretty much thumbing his nose at all of us. One of the things I have a hard time with is the fact that this man lived down the street from the very place my grown son now lives, and my grandfather Lyman Smith Senior is buried. JJD drove past the cemetery where Lyman Jones Smith is buried and I bet he knew it. The victims of rape from Citrus Heights and Rancho Cordova in particular were justified in worrying that this masked marauder could once again show up in their yard, peep in their windows all the while getting away with that, and getting away with all of the murders of not only the victims known to us, but the ones we have yet to discover.

Sometimes after researching where this man was, and he was everywhere connected to these many crimes, sometimes I can only sit and try not to feel the conflicting emotions I have about the fact that because of the times it was, and partially because rape was not seen as important or as despicable yet, that this man knew he could get away with it, and he knew he could live among us.

It will take quite a long time before we know the story that Law Enforcement is now putting together. They are on JJD's trail as they put together the evidence of where this man lived and worked over the span of Forty-Two Years. I will attempt to start the story as we know so far in the early summer of 2018. As the story evolves I am writing this book. JJD has been in jail now for a little over 4 months and now 5 months as I write what I know so far. This is also what many of you sleuth's and media hounds also know.

In the beginning we waited for the redacted documents from JJD's arrest warrant. These documents are most interesting and I like many others are glad the Judge in Sacramento decided to release them to the public. Those of us who thought the Visalia Ransacker and the East Area Rapist were/are one and the same man now have a much better idea that Law Enforcement feels the same way as they state in the warrant for JJD's arrest. There were many Law Enforcement people over time that denied any connection or who were doubtful of this connection. To me it made sense. The Visalia Ransacker stopped prowling and breaking and entering and approximately six months later he shows up in Sacramento. Visalia was his practice for what was to come.

There are 123 pages of information that were released to the public after JJD's arrest which entail the suspected murders of Brian and Katie Maggiore talks about the attacks on people in Sacramento assaults and other crimes are stated in the warrant including the murders of Lyman and Charlene Smith.

> "You see what power is
> Holding someone else's fear in our hand
> And Showing it to them" – Amy Tan

Excerpts taken from Murder On His Mind:

"On February 7, 2016 I called retired law enforcement to ask a few questions and to firm up a time and date to get together to discuss this case. I wanted to tell him what conclusion I had come to about this perpetrator. I said "I believe that this man is still alive and that he is not incarcerated and he has never been locked up. I think he is like BTK and is sitting back having stopped doing what would get him caught. I think he is enjoying his life thinking he has gotten away with raping and murdering. And he has. I think he is likely from Sacramento and that if we go back to Sacramento we will likely be more able to solve the question of who did these things."

He agreed with me completely. I came to these conclusions independently after weighing the crime reports from news articles, the brazen way this man was, and also the fact that he was aware enough of forensic science and the advances coming that he should stop what he was doing hoping the trail would go cold. I think that at this point he does not think anyone will truly take the time to track him down."

**Comments now:**

As we now know these comments were true. Especially the part about JJD thinking he had gotten away with raping and murdering. JJD did think the trail had gone cold. He thought he could continue to live among us as the clock ran out on his life. He truly did not think they would find the "needle in the haystack" Likely he thought he was too far removed from the DNA profile he had left behind. He did not think anyone of his immediate family had deposited their DNA with any of the genealogy sites. He probably thought that this was true and so he felt without that he would never be discovered. He also likely knew if he was even aware of the controversy, that the privacy laws of the main sites like Ancestry and others that help track family members would protect him from discovery.

**Back to my comments and predictions from Murder On His Mind:**

"I think this person had a fairly normal family and childhood at least from what others could see from the outside. What went on at home behind closed doors is anybody's guess. Likely he had issues with both parents. Possibly his father was a very, very strict disciplinarian and he had a mother who watched without doing anything to stop what discipline was handed out. It could be that she too was rather harsh or just did not really connect with her son. I also think that this child's birth order is that he was the oldest son and likely had at least two siblings that consisted of a sister and brother. He probably shouldered the brunt of his parents' anger throughout his childhood. I would also imagine this person likely felt inferior because he never could please his parents or anyone. At least this would have been his perception."

**Comments Now**: Of particular interest in these comments is my correct conclusion that JJD had issues with both parents. I think my conclusions in the above paragraphs have turned out to be pretty accurate. Articles I have read tell of a mother who was strict and not connected while Joseph Senior was a disciplinarian as well. He went on to remarry later on after divorcing JJD's mother, had another family that he named the same names as his first family.

**Another paragraph from my profile from Murder On His Mind:**

"The Original Night Stalker likely stopped killing in 1986 as far as we know. If he didn't really stop he likely committed crimes when he travelled, but not often. I have not heard of any killings in the United States with the same MO. Because this perpetrator learned as he went in the commission of his crimes I would not be surprised to learn that he evolved and changed his MO if he decided to commit further crimes after 1986. Some crimes in the country I have heard about were close or similar, but the perpetrator was caught. This man was so young when he committed these crimes that by 1986 he was probably 31 – 38 years old. He likely got married, had a family and tries to live within that context. I think he may still be experiencing difficulties having any real long term relationships. He has most likely been divorced more than once because the woman leaves him. Hard to say though depending on the woman he chose. If he chose a wife who is rather subservient and compliant and if he is the one in control and in charge, then this marriage might be working for him"

**My Comments Now:** What I have said was also correct as he tried to have a family and live within that context. It has come as a surprise that his wife appeared to be anything but subservient. A strong working woman was not what I expected, but as one thinks about his choices he likely married her as a model after his own mother. A strong working woman. I will leave it there as his wife is entitled to privacy and respect until or if we hear otherwise. Also, regarding his age I had always wanted him to be on the younger end of the spectrum so I thought based on descriptions from victims he was younger. His actions also made me think he was less mature. His actual age in 1986 was about 41.

**Speculation from Murder On His Mind about Real Estate:**

"This enabled him to have time to stalk his victims. If he wasn't in school, it is my belief that he or they had a relative who lived in Southern California."

Also I think that a real estate connection can be made based on his MO and his interest in homes that were for sale. I think he had access to real estate listings and knew which homes were occupied as well as more information that real estate agents would."

**My comments now:** JJD and Sharon had real estate in Sacramento. Interestingly Bonnie was in real estate. In addition, JJD did have relatives in Southern CA

There is a real estate connection within his family.

**Construction comments from Murder On His Mind:**

"Many have considered the possibility that this man worked in construction and this could be the reason for his mobility. I do not wholly agree. His hands were many times described as soft or not calloused. I suppose it is possible that he was working part time in this endeavor, but he was not seriously working full time in any career yet in my opinion. I think either he or a sibling (his brother) possibly moved to a University in Southern California and so he was able to move about freely in the night time. This enabled him to have time to stalk his victims. If he wasn't in school, it is my belief that he or they had a relative who lived in Southern California."

We do know that JJD had relatives in Southern CA and that they lived very close to Manuela Witthuhn and Janelle Cruz murder sites in Irvine CA along with possible other crimes within the same area.

**And finally my comments now:**

We shall see how much these comments will bear out, but as I mentioned I will not be surprised in the slightest to learn that JJD travelled and killed elsewhere in the United States as well as finding out who or where he may have killed after 1986. It is my belief that he killed specifically in the fall of 1988. I am extremely interested to track his whereabouts the entire year of 1988, but in particular in October and November 1988. It is my belief that JJD killed or at the very least stalked and attacked a woman alone during this time frame. His behaviors were predictable and repeated over and over. In particular, one must note that JJD was married November 10, 1973 to Sharon Huddle. We know that he attacked and raped a female on his anniversary for at least two years in a row – November 10, 1976 and November 10, 1977. Dates, anniversaries and his life events are completely connected to when he acted out. They meant something to him and it seems they triggered his attacking in the same months or even the same dates.

There seems to be a time fram that JJD is harder to track between 1980 and 1990. I believe he was off the grid as much as possible as this was when JJD was laying low. He was also a father of three young children during this time frame. His wife was likely the breadwinner

## Chapter Six

## Why was he not caught in the beginning?

If we completely ignore Mr. DeAngelo's activities while an Exeter Police Officer, if we pretend none of these prowling's and burglaries occurred by a perpetrator known as the Visalia Ransacker and only look at JJD's activities while he was in Auburn PD we will find an officer worthy of a second look. I know that many have complained about law enforcement. I certainly have been up and down with my reactions to the fact that a police officer was committing such horrendous crimes in Sacramento and elsewhere WHILE he was actively working to supposedly protect our communities from evil men such as himself.

I have not wanted to complain or chastise current Law Enforcement in any way about what they could do nothing about. These crimes happened 42 years ago and previously. I have to get this off my chest however. So, forgive me while I say my piece. Then I will do my best to let it go.

Hindsight truly is 20/20, but! bear with me on this for a moment. Recognizing that jurisdictions did not cooperate with one another back in the 1970's this police officer knew he could come and go as he pleased across any jurisdiction while they all scratched their heads and debated whether or not this was or could be the same guy. But, here's the thing, this man was attacking women and terrorizing communities EVERYWHERE he went. ALL of the jurisdictions were aware of his attacks, his MO and his travels. They discussed this criminal amongst themselves for the better part of 2 years in Sacramento alone. When EAR showed up in Contra Costa county Sacramento warned them that EAR was coming their way.

Looking at EAR alone and the attacks just in Sacramento, not looking at anything else we can see that this man was/is a sophisticated perp. The investigators of the times could see that he was not going to stop. As EAR travelled through the different jurisdictions, as he left moving on from place to place each county was relieved he had moved on. They sometimes told their investigators as they dismantled their rape task forces not to worry about it. He was gone; he was no longer their problem. This type of thinking especially as it surrounded "Just" a rapist is why and how this man was not only allowed to be free, but he was allowed to evolve into a serial killer/rapist. On closer examination the bottom line was about the cost involved within departments to continue a rape task force, a harsh reality then.

In the 1970's, and previously the attitude about rape in society, in our communities, was one of avoidance, and also rape was seen as a lesser crime. Rapists did not see the possible consequences of such a crime as a deterrent. The punishments for possible rapists to consider were minimal. The rape kits submitted into evidence sat on shelves many times untested forever.

Little by little, inch by inch things have improved when it comes to trying to impose stiffer penalties for would be rapists. Just last year in the State of California the statute of limitations was removed so that the crime of rape can be prosecuted forever just like murder is.

One has to ask the questions about the timing involved with the arrest finally of Joseph DeAngelo. One has to wonder why now? Why not three years ago, why not ten years ago? Why all of the delays, inactivity, back burner time frames by each jurisdiction? Why was there or why did there appear to be a malaise or an apathy a huge delay – like watching paint dry. I visualize the lag in time as though there are many people standing around looking at one another, waiting. Waiting for what? What timing were they waiting for? The question is asked in relationship to current times. The last decade truly was more in line with being able to actually find the criminal because of advances in technology. I also recognize that in the real world back in the 1970's in particular that every detective worked on cases knowing that the lack of equipment, budget problems and a shortage of manpower played an important role in the problems facing them. I am certain solving crimes especially back then was a difficult task. The departments were all in the midst of change, huge changes in everything they had done before.

## The CREEP Among Us * Anne Penn

I write this without having had the answers to the questions I am asking. I have spoken to different members of the Law Enforcement community and so far have asked a few of the people who worked the case those many years ago. I still want more information, more details about this. I need to hear what their theory on these questions might be. As a victim family member the last three years in particular were excruciatingly long and frustrating. So much so that I had to write the book Murder On His Mind. I tried to get the word out to the people in Sacramento. I went onto 1970's sites in Sacramento. I tried to tell whoever would listen that I thought the perp was in Sacramento and had been virtually all along. All of these years.

I spoke to Paul Belli, Paul Holes, Mark Knudsen. and others. Besides the difficult wait I have to say one of the things that was most disturbing about finding out this guy truly was always in Sacramento and surrounding areas, and finding out that I was correct in thinking he was Law Enforcement (I thought he became a cop after the attacks seemed to have stopped). What was disturbing was finding out he was actively working as LE while he was attacking. What better cover than that? The third thing that was disturbing to discover was that he was in the very same areas he had attacked and that he not only was and is a dangerous man. He could have been prowling, stalking, breaking in and continuing to terrorize the good people of Citrus Heights, Roseville and Rancho Cordova unfettered for 30 plus years. What an outrage.

## The CREEP Among Us * Anne Penn

We may never be able to prove that he continued prowling after 1979 in Sacramento, but there are police reports of prowling's. There are stories of his stalking, and breaking in. I have included Sue's story which happened in 1983 in this book. There are reports that are likely JJD after 1980 doing just that and continuing to terrorize the Sacramento, Citrus Heights, Rancho Cordova victims. He had stayed in their neighborhoods, shopping at the local Bel Air market, eating at the local diner. JJD was among them watching them, watching their children. We have not yet connected him to more murders in Sacramento County. We may yet discover there are more bodies to be counted. But, what we do know is that JJD stayed put. He was right there a stone's throw away from all of the addresses of the many, many victims he had once hurt emotionally, physically, psychologically and more those many years ago. He was allowed to live among them taking his pleasure at that very idea and more.

I know that the detectives who initially caught these cases to investigate in 1976 and after did the best job they could at the time with procedures and investigative tools available then. They had to work from the directive of those in charge of their agencies, but the reality is they did not catch him, they did not stop him. JJD AKA EAR, and the Visalia Ransacker continued on arrogantly and without any fear himself. He knew they could not and would not catch him. He knew – I stress these words; HE KNEW he was free to do whatever he decided. He knew that he was at least two steps or in many cases more steps ahead of the investigators in every jurisdiction because he knew how they worked, and what their weaknesses were. He knew from his training, his education and his experience that the jurisdictions would not cooperate with one another. He knew even if it was not in the training manual that the reality of police work especially back in their day was they would not share information easily. This is the first reason JJD was not caught.

The final arrest of JJD was finely orchestrated for all the world to see. The arrest came right after every show had been seen on television. It came after the cases had been promoted in the media at long last the way they should have been many, many years ago. For the last 2 plus years ID channel, Oxygen, HLN, 48 hours, and more reported on the Original Night Stalker. Make no mistake this did not occur because of one author, or one article written. This occurred because this was the narrative that Law Enforcement orchestrated for all of the public to see. The FBI was brought back into the cases to garner national attention. Every single drop of information was controlled and put out into the world inch by inch, and until LE and the media were ready the arrest or other real information was not given.

For the last two years especially I kept wondering why the delay? They knew they could solve it with his DNA profile. What was taking so long? A podcast was done not long ago given in depth by Sheriff's Detective Ken Clark about the reasons they thought the Maggiore Murders really were the work of EAR. In very great detail Sheriff Clark talks about the Maggiore murders which took place in February 1978. So much of what had been told before this interview was confusing to almost all who tried to figure out who saw what. How many perps, who had what on them, in their pocket, were there really two guys or shoe laces on the ground? What weapon was used and was it EAR or if they thought it was EAR why then the big investigation at Mather Air Force Base where they looked at crimes by drug dealers and military?

Sheriff's Detective Ken Clark attempts to answer all the questions. Ken Clark was not involved in the original investigations and as I have said I am grateful that over the years as investigators retired that this case was passed along to the next detectives who came along with new fresh eyes to try and determine who the perpetrator was. During the recent podcast in 2018 we are told that they (he) looked at all the files again in detail, and low and behold after all these years the story somehow could be sorted out and was in the files all along. It was EAR who killed the Maggiore's. So here is what happened:

Over time and when Sheriff's Detective Ken Clark arrived as part of the cold case team which was the most recent past, is he was able to collect all of the old reports and learn about many things that had not previously been passed to the EAR Task Force those many years ago. DeAngelo was arrested for the Maggiore murder's in Sacramento County April

2018. He was charged with these murders and so could be housed in Sacramento County and now he will be tried there. The answers were always in Sacramento. Once again, the way things were done in the past seemed to obstruct from view all of the information to help solve the cases. Unfortunately, divisions did not always give information to other divisions who were not involved in the investigation.

I am certain I am not the only one from Sacramento who was there in the 1970's along with the many, many victims as well as community members who thought this man was still there all this time. I know for a fact that Larry Crompton was of the same mind. I had come to him on the phone one day to tell him that after I had spent time investigating this individual, and these crimes that I knew EAR he was still there in Sacramento. It was February 2016. So, if amateur sleuths could figure out the odds of this serial killer still being in Sacramento why did investigators not seem to know it? Maybe they did. The information stayed with them if they had any idea.

I will attempt to lay this out from articles, news reports from the times and any shred of information I can find in order to try to answer this question.

Working from the reports in August 1979 and newspaper articles we know that DeAngelo was working in Auburn as a police officer. He was arrested in July 1979 for shoplifting. If we only looked at this one issue, this one red flag by itself based on the fact that he was arrested in Sacramento

County during the time frames of attacks, and in the very areas that EAR was attacking why was this man not looked at, seriously looked at for the crimes of EAR? Would it have been that hard to keep an eye on him? Sacramento County knew EAR, his MO, his travels, his stalking habits and just about all you could know (I would hope). EAR had left Sacramento County for all intents and purposes in April of 1978. He moved on attacking other counties, Contra Costa was one as he continued his reign of terror throughout 1979. DeAngelo was aware that Sacramento County came close to him in 1978. That is one of the reasons he moved on. The Maggiore murders composites had come close to how he looked at the time as a cop in Auburn CA. If they never connected the rapist as also the murderer of the Maggiore's at the time, if Sacramento County only thought EAR was a rapist, they were glad he had moved on. He was gone from their jurisdiction. He was not their concern any longer.

The behavior of Sacramento County at the time would indicate that they truly only thought of EAR as a rapist. I say this because of what they did with the rape kits and the rape reports during the next few years. Rape had a statute of limitations of about 4 years from 1976-1979 time frames of his activity in Sacramento. In the case of say rape victim #5 Jane Carson Sandler who was lucky enough to at least have had a female detective to speak to in the person of Carol Daly, in her case Jane was raped in 1976. They would have kept her rape kit and only been obligated by law to keep the kit for four or five years.

The rape kits were probably never tested and were thrown out between 1981-1984. They followed the law at that time. The reports were passed around from Sac County. I have heard retired detective Richard Shelby had the files for a long time and then eventually gave them back to Sac County. What I am saying here is that if Sac County truly thought that the mass rapist and terrorist was also a murderer in 1978 why then would they get rid of files and get rid of rape kit evidence? When the crimes were eventually connected by DNA in about 2000 it was only accomplished because Contra Costa County had kept some of their rape kits and had kept their files on the East Area Rapist. Contra Costa had kept their information and evidence for more than 20 years at the time the DNA was then tested against that of the kits taken from murder scenes down in Southern CA. All could have been connected back at that time if Santa Barbara County had been cooperating with other jurisdictions. They finally allowed testing to be done on their evidence in about 2006. That in itself is a question – what did they have to lose by checking it out? Sooner?

The CREEP Among Us * Anne Penn

## Auburn Policeman Faces Disiplinary Procedure

8/22/79
AUG 5

Disciplinary action is being considered against an Auburn policeman who was cited last month in Sacramento County on charges of shoplifting.

Joseph DeAngelo was cited July 21 for allegedly attempting to steal a hammer and can of dog repellant from the Pay N Save store off Greenback Lane in Citrus Heights.

According to Sacramento County Sheriff's reports, DeAngelo was caught with the items by store employees and cited by Sheriff's deputies.

City Manager Jack Sausser Friday said DeAngelo has been suspended from duty with pay and city officials are currently investigating the allegations against him.

Sausser has been interviewing persons involved with the incident but no decision has been made regarding DeAngelo's job with the city.

If a policeman is fired, he has 15 days to appeal the decision before the city's Personnel Appeals Board in a public hearing.

City Attorney Richard Prather said the investigation was a personnel matter and declined to comment.

DeAngelo Monday had no comment on the allegations, nor did his Chico attorney, Maurene Wheland.

Auburn Police Chief Nick Willick also had no comment on the allegations other than the matter was being investigated.

In 1979

## Auburn Policeman Dismmissed In Shoplifting Accusation

Joseph DeAngelo, the Auburn policeman accused of shoplifting a can of dog repellant and a hammer at a Sacramento drug store last month, was fired this week.

Auburn City Manager Jack Sausser said DeAngelo failed to answer any of the city's investigations and did not request an administrative hearing so was dismissed Monday.

"There was justifiable grounds to remove him from the public sector," Sausser said Monday.

DeAngelo, who is represented by Chico attorney Maurene Wheland, was not available for comment.

Auburn Police Chief Nick Willick Tuesday said, "It is very important that the community have the utmost trust and faith in its officers' integrity; when this trust and faith has been compromised, officers can no longer effectively function in the community."

According to Willick, as a result of an investigation into DeAngelo's fitness and conduct, the city has determined that dismissal was warranted.

DeAngelo was cited by Sacramento County Sheriff's deputies for allegedly shoplifting July 21, at the Pay N' Save Store off Greenback Lane in Citrus Heights.

According to Sheriff's reports, DeAngelo was caught trying to steal the items by store employees.

DeAngelo has 15 days to file a formal appeal to the city's 5-member Personnel Appeals Board.

What this article states from August 29, 1979 from the Auburn Journal is this:

Joseph DeAngelo, the Auburn policeman accused of shoplifting a can of dog repellant and a hammer at a Sacramento drug store last month, was fired this week.

The CREEP Among Us * Anne Penn

## Jury Finds Policeman Guilty Of Shoplifting

OCT 31 1979   AUg 7

Joseph DeAngelo, former Auburn policman, was found guilty of misdemeanor shoplifting charges by a Sacramento County jury Friday.

He was given a $100 fine and six months probation, by Sacramento Municipal Court Judge Thomas Daugherty.

DeAngelo was fired from the police force shortly after his arrest last July 2, at the Pay N' Save store off Greenback Lane.

His Chico attorney, Maureen Whelan, Tuesday was unavailable for comment on the status of the appeal, but it will be heard Nov. 9 before the Auburn Personnel Board.

During the three-day trial, a store employee testified he saw DeAngelo take a can of dog repellant from the waistband of his trousers. Another employee told jurors that he pulled a hammer from DeAngelo's trousers.

DeAngelo took the stand Thursday afternoon and denied he was trying to steal the items.

What these articles tell us in a nutshell is this: DeAngelo was in Sacramento at a Pay N Save store off Greenback. Greenback is not far from the areas of attack for EAR. This crime occurred in July 1979. JJD was immediately fired from the Auburn Police Department. The article states that DeAngelo was cited by Sacramento County Sheriff's deputies for allegedly shoplifting items from the store on Greenback which as most of us from Sacramento know is in Citrus Heights. Did he look even remotely like any of the composites of EAR of the times? Did anyone at all who read the articles from

Sacramento or Auburn even have the inkling of the thought that maybe DeAngelo should be looked at as a suspect to the East Area Rapist crimes? Why was he not looked at in 1979? I absolutely have to ask that question. As a victim family member I truly have to ask why he was not looked at in 1979.

He was not on anyone's list is what Sacramento County DA said during the public statement read to us as communities on April 25, 2018, the afternoon of the day that Joseph James DeAngelo was booked into the Sacramento County jail. Forty-Two years, after the first attacks by the East Area Rapist.

All who read this have to allow me this rant about the fact that JJD was allowed to roam free 38 years after the murders of my uncle Lyman Robert Smith and his beautiful wife Charlene. Other victims' family members must wonder if their loved ones might have been saved had JJD been looked at with suspicion in 1979 as a possible EAR suspect. Why was this not done? And we know it was not done. We know that JJD was not on anyone's list until six days before his arrest. That is what we were told. And, even if protocol changed over time, it would seem that in the last twenty years their openness to look at their own could possibly have found the perp. It just made sense. As the public we do not have access to the records from Sac County and other surrounding counties into officer issues. It made sense to go back and look at any LE officer who had been fired, who had emotional or mental health issues. If the public had any access to records such as these Joseph James DeAngelo would have been on the suspect list long, long ago.

In the summer of 1979 there were several articles about the arrest and prosecution of Joseph James DeAngelo. Not one, but several. Hmmm. Yet not a peep from LE about this man who was as it turns out the perfect suspect especially in 1979. I wish I had read the paper everyday back then. Hindsight. To be fair, I truly can see how he was missed in every department and in every jurisdiction.

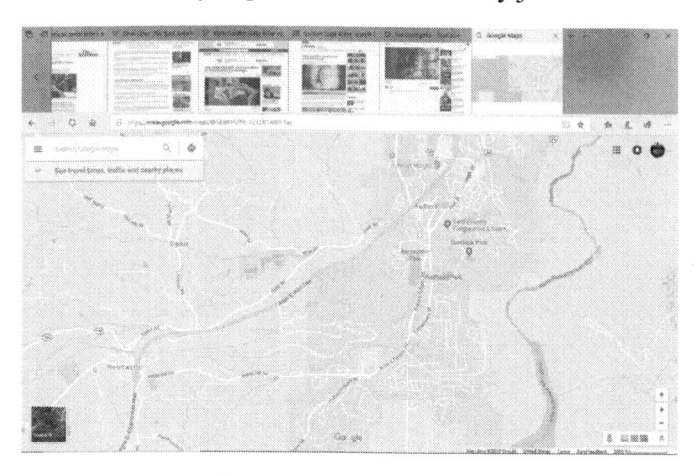

The next couple of maps show just how easy it was to travel from Auburn where DeAngelo was working to Citrus Heights and all of the East Area neighborhoods of Sacramento where he attacked and prowled. Note that on this map the city of Auburn is north of Sacramento. One can travel the Highway 80 freeway, but that is not as much fun and is less direct than if one takes the Auburn Folsom Road. Note that immediately south of Auburn is the Auburn Folsom

Road which is a country road really. Or at least it used to be in the 1970's. JJD lived in Auburn area when he first came to California from Bath New York. Note the next picture of the map that continues south.

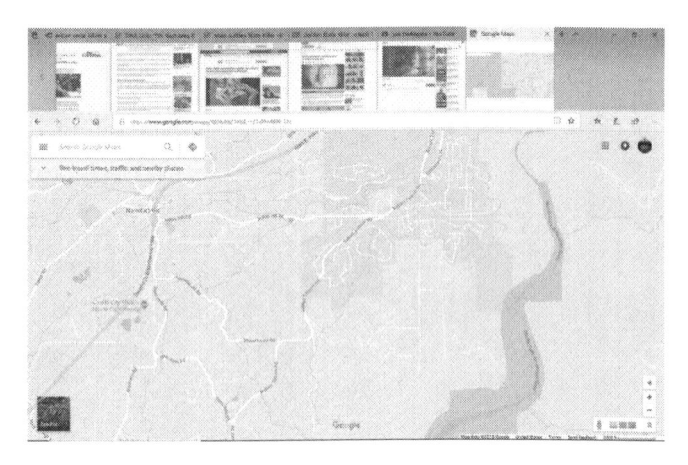

Note that as you take the Auburn Folsom Road South you pass Indian Hill Road continuing south as this road runs parallel along Highway 80 South. At the bottom of this snapshot of the map you see Newcastle Road. To the right you can see the North Fork of the American River. For better views yourself go to google maps and follow the road and his path yourself.

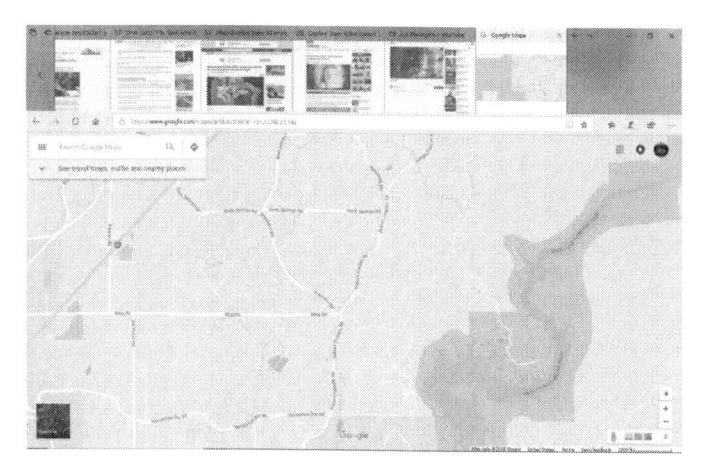

Continuing South on Auburn-Folsom Road the farthest road south shown here is Horseshoe Bar Road. And we continue to see the North Fork of the American River. And as we continue South see next map you can see that Auburn Folsom Road is a very long uninterrupted way to travel from Auburn to East Sacramento.

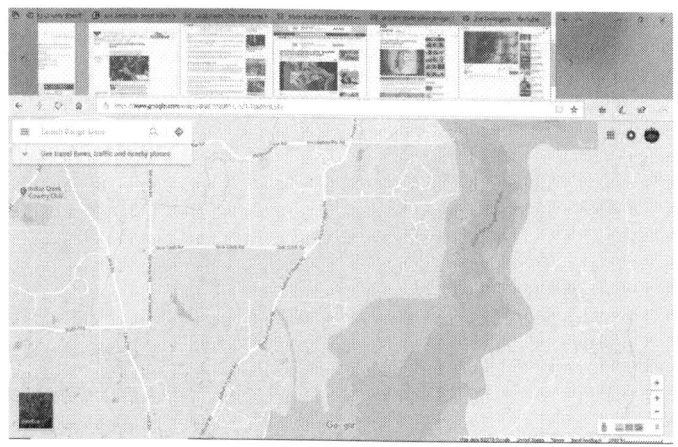

The Auburn Folsom Road continues South into granite Bay and towards Folsom Lake along the west side of the lake. Eventually one drops down into Roseville and East Sacramento neighborhoods.

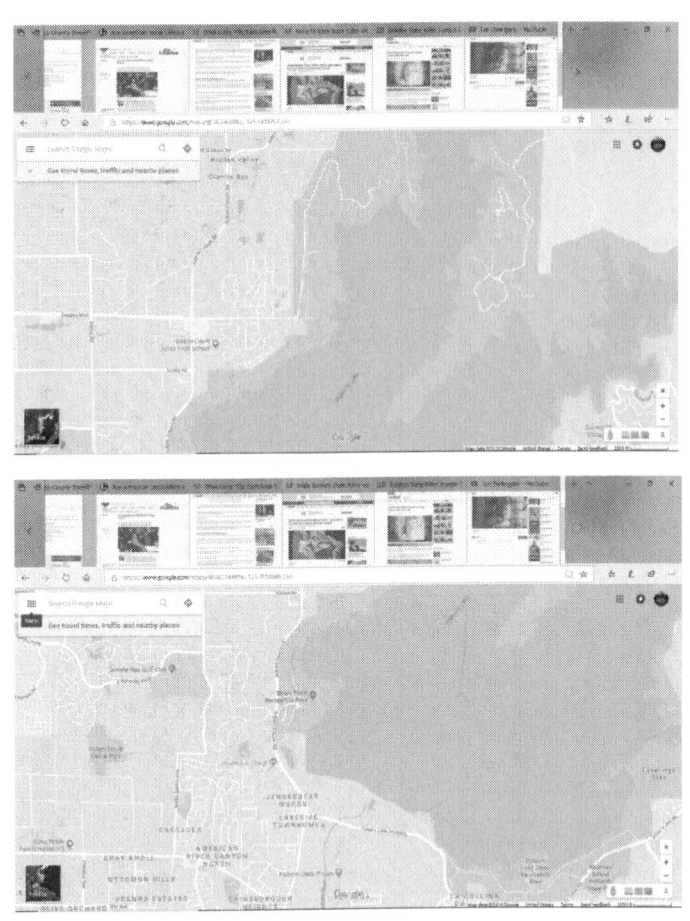

From here JJD could cut over to Old Auburn Blvd, or Douglas Blvd. One of many ways to cut over to Citrus Heights. JJD knew all the back roads for several reasons. One is if you go to Sierra College, and JJD did this used to be out in the country. It is a pleasant drive rather than taking any highway and it more direct running as the crow flies. If you google map yourself everything I have stated here you can see how simple it was for JJD to leave work, jump on Auburn Folsom to arrive in 20 minutes to his intended target area. Easy to do reconnaissance, prowl and eventually attack the target. He could drive back to Auburn if he was living there at the time. Auburn is where JJD married Sharon Huddle in a church not far from where I had my own wedding. He married Sharon in 1973 in Auburn. He moved to Exeter for three years and then came back to Auburn. He worked there until 1979. Attacked in Sacramento until Spring 1978. Then he attacked one more time in 1979 in Rancho Cordova. This attack was March 20, 1979. This was prior to his arrest and firing in July 1979 from the Auburn Police Department. After that his attacks were mostly out of this area.

Of note on the next map is the Old Auburn Blvd. which crosses Sierra College Blvd. and can take you to the Sierra College he attended at one time. Also note that when they arrested JJD on Canyon Oaks Drive that the nearest street out of his neighorhood and of the home purchased in 1980 was Auburn Folsom Road. This entire area was easy to get to through the back country roads of the times with little traffic. It is important to note that when real estate was purchased off Canyon Oaks JJD truly was living in the attack areas along side his victims

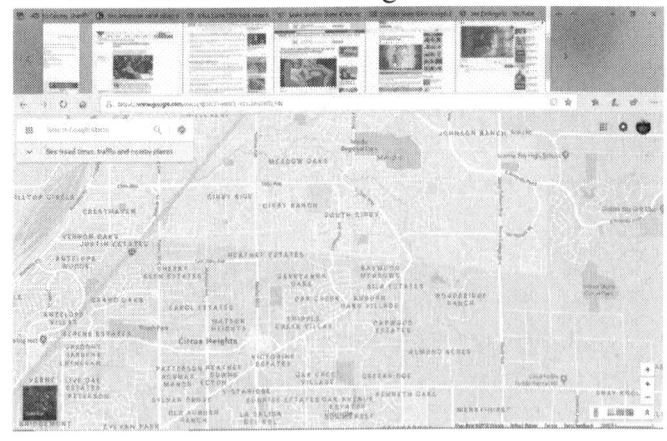

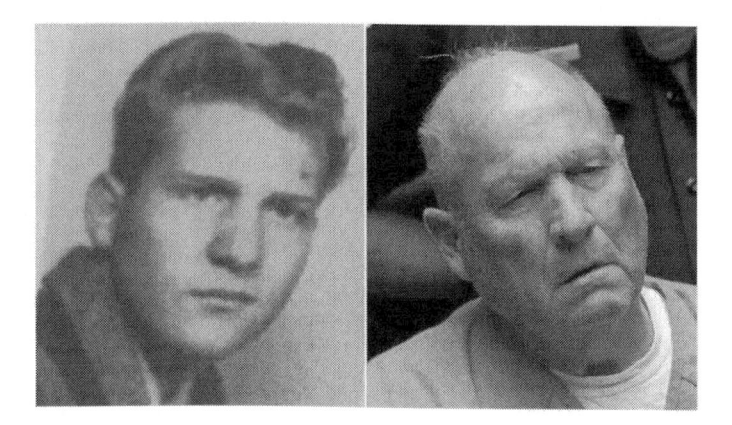

You can see the issues behind his eyes from the beginning. Joseph James DeAngelo in High School (left) and right being arraigned in court April 2018.

The CREEP in a cage at last.

Composite drawn after the Maggiore murders and the one the FBI was using in 2016.

In 2007 an episode of Dexter called "That Night a Forest Grew" was the show. In the story, The Law Enforcement Officers who worked the case of the Bay Harbor Butcher are shown discussing a manifesto sent to them by who they think is the perpetrator. The FBI was called in; the local department had been working the case. The two departments plus special agents had all read the manifesto. The perp who we all would know was actually Dexter, a Forensic Scientist/Criminalist with the department. Dexter got different parts of his manifesto from blogs as he created a paper which included Political, Environmental, Religious, some things about Berlin Germany, Julius Caesar, the Pittsburg Steelers and finally Gandhi.

As all involved are shown discussing the manifesto they all come back at one another with completely different theories of who the guy could possibly be, they are shown talking over one another. One of the characters says "This is what he wants, confusion, chaos, it's what the killer wants. He's always been an intensely private figure dispatching victims silently – now he's suddenly a media whore? It doesn't make sense." The FBI man's next statement is "You know what that means?" He walks over to a chalkboard where he writes in capital letters "LAW ENFORCEMENT BACKGROUND." "He knows how we work. Look how he hits every major theme. It's called scatter shock. He knew that this would send us scurrying like squirrels for nuts.

Another character says "Yeah but to suggest he might be one of us – how can you be sure?"

This reminds me of everyone scurrying around trying to decipher the papers supposedly dropped near a crime scene early on by JJD/EAR that is titled Mad is The Word, as well as a report about General Custer. Even better a map was dropped that Paul Holes spent a ton of time trying to decipher what neighborhood is depicted in the drawing. Somehow people believed these papers actually meant something. EAR sent a poem to the media in Sacramento called Excitements Crave early on. JJD had to laugh at all of the scurrying that was done when news of the papers came out as well as originally when the poem was sent to the media long, long ago.

I did not spend time trying to figure out these papers because I wanted proof they had actually come from the perp. I asked, "was his DNA on the papers?" Did we know for a fact that these had come from EAR? "Did you find any epithelial cells on them that matches the DNA profile left?" I said "Until we know for a FACT these papers came from EAR I don't see the value of them" If they did test the papers likely nothing was found like sweat, skin cells or anything else. JJD was trying to create what one character from Dexter called a cluster fuck. (I don't cuss, but it seems appropriate to quote it as written in this case). The cluster was successful. The tactics used early on were textbook what EAR had learned in Law Enforcement training. His degree in

Criminal Justice, his internship, his on the job experience all told him that he was smarter and that he truly could get away with anything he wanted to. Including murder. JJD had no crystal ball in which to see the future. He made one mistake in leaving bodily fluids behind. Otherwise we would still be looking for that needle in the haystack. And likely JJD would have died in the next decade or so never being identified.

Old fashioned police work could have caught JJD back in the beginning as I say IF ONLY they had looked at their own. There was a trail then, but it was a trail that was only visible to those who did not look at this with the naked eye. It was visible like a thread, like Harry Potter with his invisible cloak, JJD hid right in front of us, but Law Enforcement could have seen him. They should have seen him back then. Visalia suspected EAR was their guy, they suspected The Visalia Ransacker had murdered Claude Snelling. They tried to tell Sacramento County of their suspicions and were blown off. Sacramento County arrested JJD for stealing right in the attack zone of the East Area Rapist. He was a cop. They knew it. They also knew he worked in Auburn and knew the area of EAR. He was arrested in the EAR attack neighborhoods in 1979. Do you see the invisible trail that could have been seen by Law Enforcement? JJD used his position as a police officer knowing that he would have an invisible cloak or shield from all of us, and then in the end he knew that the cloak would also shield him from Law Enforcement. Ah…. But hindsight is so clear.

All we had to do after all those years was watch an episode of Dexter back in 2007. Maybe we could have saved the extra decade of waiting for all of the victims and their families.

Of course now in 2018 he would have a much harder time getting away with anything. Ted Bundy and many other criminals from the 1970's had old procedures used in Law Enforcement to try and find them. Everything has changed for the new criminals in 2018.

## Chapter Seven

## The Murder Victims

DeAngelo has been charged with the murder of Professor Claude Snelling. As far as we know Professor Snelling was the first murder victim of JJD.

Professor Snelling was robbed of his ability to watch and enjoy as his daughter grew up. He did the most noble thing in giving his life to possibly save hers. He certainly was a hero in his final moments on earth.

Sgt. Brian Maggiore and Katie Maggiore murdered in Rancho Cordova 1978.

The slayings of an Air Force Sergeant and his wife, who were gunned down in the backyard of a Rancho Cordova home February 2, may have been committed by two young men, a spokesman for the sheriff's department said today.

Along with the announcement composite sketches of the two suspects, made from a neighbor's description, were released.

Sgt. Brian Maggiore, 21, and his wife Katie, 20 were accosted while walking their dog and shot to death at the rear of a home on La Gloria Drive in Rancho Cordova.

William Miller, assistant to the sheriff, said two young men were seen on La Gloria minutes before the shooting. One was wearing a brown leather type jacket gathered at the waist with a zippered front, small collar and dark stain on the back. He was also wearing brown pointed boots. The other man was wearing a dark jacket, zippered in front with slash pockets, dark pants and black shoes or boots. He was also wearing brown leather gloves, Miller said. **END OF ARTICLE**

**April 24, 2018 DeAngelo was charged with the murders of Brian and Katie Maggiore in Rancho Cordova in Sacramento. It is believed these murders were self-preservation murders because the two had seen DeAngelo peeping or in some act of prowling and it is believed he was not wearing**

**his ski mask. If the young couple saw DeAngelo's face that was all that was required for him to chase the young couple down and shoot them until they were dead. It is now believed as reported from Sheriff's Detective Ken Clark from Sacramento County that there were never two men involved in these two murders.** Note - Update:

In 2018 Criminology Podcast by Mike Morford https://criminology.libsyn.com/ with Sheriff Ken Clark from Sacramento County . The interview is in great detail explaining why Joseph James DeAngelo was a suspect as EAR, and why he has been charged upon his arrest with the murders of Brian and Katie Maggiore on February 2, 1978.

The CREEP Among Us * Anne Penn

Katie and Brian Maggiore

Sacramento County homicide investigators Friday said they had no leads or suspects in the gunshot deaths of a young Rancho Cordova Air Force sergeant and his wife.

Brian K. Maggiore, 21, and Katie Maggiore, 20, were gunned down Thursday night by a man who apparently confronted them as they walked their dog along a quiet residential street.

The CREEP Among Us * Anne Penn

Debra Alexandria Manning (Bottom)
Dr. Robert Offerman (Top)

The CREEP Among Us * Anne Penn

A Goleta Valley orthopedic surgeon and a Santa Maria clinical psychologist believed to be his girlfriend were found murdered yesterday in his condominium on Avenida Pequena, sheriff's deputies reported.

Dr. Robert J. Offerman, 41, and Dr. Debra (Dee) Alexandria Manning, 35, were found dead at 11:33 a.m. in the bedroom of Offerman's residence at 767 Avenida Pequena, detectives said. Detective William Baker said that both victims had been shot to death. Time of death was tentatively set at about 3:00 a.m. Sunday. Neighbors had heard shots, Baker said, but didn't report them thinking they were holiday firecrackers. END OF ARTICLE

## The CREEP Among Us * Anne Penn

Lyman and Charlene Smith

The bodies of Smith, 43, and his 33-year-old wife were found Sunday, bound and beaten inside their fashionable hillside home in Ventura, by Smith's son, Gary, 12, when he went to the residence to mow the lawn.

The couple appeared to have been bludgeoned with a fireplace log that was found in the bedroom near the bodies, according to Lydick. Lydick said the log, which appeared to be covered with blood, is believed to be the weapon used to kill the Smiths.

The log is being examined at the Ventura County Sheriff's Department Crime Laboratory.

Keith and Patrice Harrington   Keith Harrington was a third year medical student and his new wife of four months was a registered nurse. Apparently ONS would watch through windows and was just outside their bedroom. Both Keith and Patrice were found with markings on their bodies indicating they had been bound. Patrice had been raped. The cord had been cut and removed. Some of it was on Keith's lower back. This was odd. Both had been bound with their hands behind their back. Both had been bludgeoned with the bedspread over their heads. The murder weapon was never found. After their assailant murdered them he must have taken down the spread, cut their bindings and just let some fall where they would. He then covered them again. Again, there was no forced entry into the house. There was another bruise on Patrice Harrington. It was "a circular contusion" on her shoulder and could be said to be consistent with a bite mark."

Manuela Witthuhn

On February 6, 1981 in Irvine California 28-year-old Manuela Witthuhn was murdered while lying on her bed. The cause of death was a skull fracture. A ball of fibers was noted on her skin at the base of her spine. This was also noted on Lyman Smith at the scene of his murder. The weapon was removed from the scene. A rear sliding glass door had pry marks and damage to the frame.

# The CREEP Among Us * Anne Penn

**Cheri Domingo and Greg Sanchez**

Sheriff's detectives are today investigating similarities between the brutal murder of a man and a woman found yesterday at 449 Toltec Way in Goleta and the nearby fatal shootings of a couple 1-1/2 years ago.

The Toltec Way victims were identified today as Cheri Domingo, 35 a divorcee who was house-sitting at the residence, and her former boyfriend, Greg Sanchez, 28. Deputies said the bodies were found about 11:30 a.m. yesterday by a real estate agent who came to look at the house. The property was put on the market three months ago after the death of the owner who was a relative of Mrs. Domingo.

**Janelle Cruz**

**The Register (Irvine, California) May 1986**

Irvine police Thursday tentatively identified the body of a woman who was found bludgeoned to death this week as 18-year-old Janelle Lisa Cruz.

The teenager was found dead Monday afternoon inside her home when a real estate agent showed the house to a prospective buyer, police Lt. Al Muir said.

An autopsy Tuesday showed Cruz died of multiple blows to the head. Muir said police were "99 percent sure" that the body is that of Cruz, but a positive identification was still being sought by the county Coroner's Office through dental records.

The CREEP Among Us * Anne Penn

# RAPIST'S TRAIL OF TERROR

The East Area Rapist is suspected of committing 30 attacks, including one murder of a couple in Sacramento County, from 1976-1978. Locations are approximate.

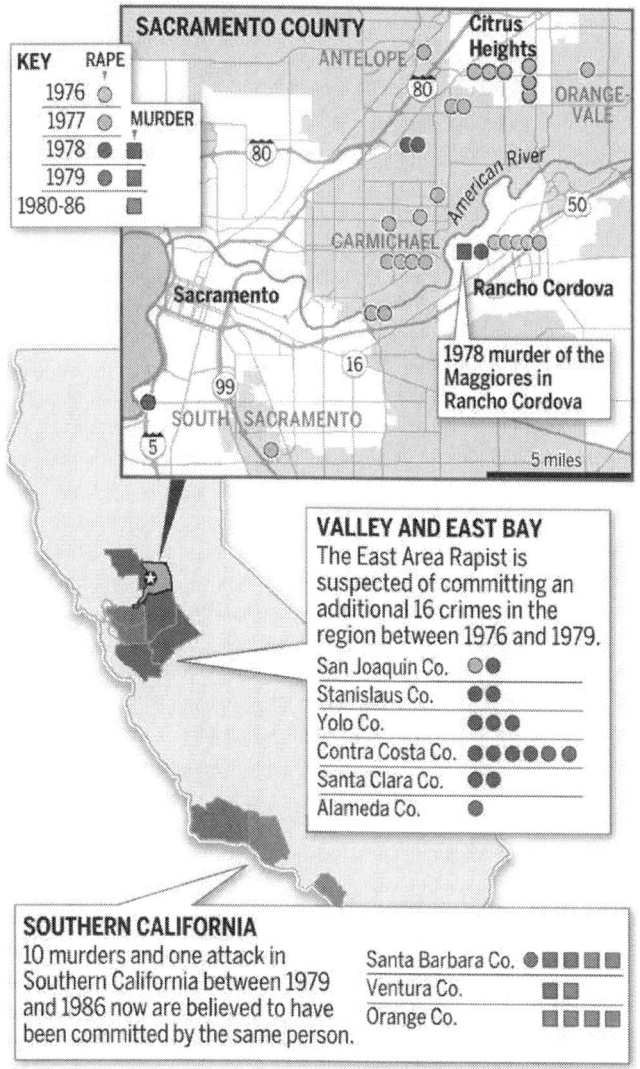

**KEY**

RAPE
- 1976 ○
- 1977 ○
- 1978 ●
- 1979 ●
- 1980-86

MURDER
- 1978 ■
- 1979 ■
- 1980-86 ■

**SACRAMENTO COUNTY**

ANTELOPE
Citrus Heights
ORANGEVALE
American River
CARMICHAEL
Sacramento
Rancho Cordova
SOUTH SACRAMENTO

1978 murder of the Maggiores in Rancho Cordova

5 miles

**VALLEY AND EAST BAY**

The East Area Rapist is suspected of committing an additional 16 crimes in the region between 1976 and 1979.

| | |
|---|---|
| San Joaquin Co. | ○● |
| Stanislaus Co. | ●● |
| Yolo Co. | ●●● |
| Contra Costa Co. | ●●●●●●● |
| Santa Clara Co. | ●● |
| Alameda Co. | ● |

**SOUTHERN CALIFORNIA**

10 murders and one attack in Southern California between 1979 and 1986 now are believed to have been committed by the same person.

| | |
|---|---|
| Santa Barbara Co. | ●■■■■ |
| Ventura Co. | ■■ |
| Orange Co. | ■■■■ |

Source: ear-ons.com          SHARON OKADA  sokada@sacbee.com

## Chapter Eight

## Lack of Cooperation

## Mistakes Made & Articles

What was true and what is not? Well these questions surrounding these cases will be difficult to answer after 42 plus years. One of the concrete things we will determine and come to know is where JJD was during the crimes. Piece by piece. Those people who worked with JJD and have given interviews sound as though they have some doubt that their friend and the person they thought they knew could possibly be the evil monster that we all know he had to be. One fishing buddy said "DNA is not always correct."

A 100% DNA match leaves little and no room for doubt. LE will and have been finding out that this man was in the areas of attack and murder. He can be placed near and in the attack zones. I cannot yet say this completely, but so far he can be placed at the appropriate times and places of the criminals travels, attacks, and murders. How do I write this before JJD has even had a fair trial? He is innocent until proven guilty in a court of law. The problem these days is the DNA evidence which does not lie. Now and into the future DNA evidence will be hard to refute. It will be difficult to hear a man who left his semen at the scene of his many crimes all those years ago try to stand up in court and say the words: "Not guilty." In the old days this may have worked depending on the defense attorney's strategy and the effective or ineffective prosecution. Proving crimes beyond a reasonable doubt has just become easier with a 100% DNA match. How can a perpetrator of evil actually expect us to believe he could possibly not be guilty when he has left what is essentially his fingerprint on the bodies of his victims? He left the same DNA trail from 1976 until at least 1986. It did not change. There is no other DNA that was left at the scenes of the crimes.

It would save all of us a lot of time and money if JJD would just take responsibility for his actions. He will be a self-survivalist until the end. So, that all being said, I have to talk about what we know of Law Enforcement at the time. I have it on very good authority that an attitude was present at least some of the time within Law Enforcement that when a call would come in for the crime of rape many did not really want to take such a call. Back in the day there was even a policy about a rape investigation in at least one jurisdiction that if a victim did not know the alleged rapist they did not investigate the crime. When one LE jurisdiction tried to warn another and tried to discuss the perp in Walnut Creek this LE investigator was told "get out we don't need your help." Another task force was being disbanded in 1979 and because the perp had left their area the statements made to the task force although the investigators knew the criminal was not done and that he was likely going to evolve into something worse they were told "He has left our area, leave it alone".

Also back in the day there were crimes committed by LE within departments such as cheating or stealing. One department fired at least 14 deputies for stealing and cheating. The public does not have access to personnel records or issues within departments. I understand privacy laws and issues. I also know that transparency when it comes to discipline and red flags that arise among individual officers should be noted. These days we do get reports about disciplinary actions taken with officers, but typically that happens when something very serious has happened in our communities. Anyone who has issues that we know about prior to them becoming serious we can take action to try to avoid a serious outcome by any behavior problems with anyone. It should not matter if it is a teacher, a coach, a school bus driver, a guy who works for the DMV or a police officer.

We always look back intensely and in as much detail as possible at a perpetrator who carries out a mass shooting. We ask how did we miss this. There were signs, there were issues. The question is, why many times do we look the other way? In the 1970's our society was a completely different animal than today. In the 1970's people did not speak, did not call the police, did not discuss personal or private issues because there could be shame involved. Many rapes went unreported for this reason. Rape victims were afraid that people would think of them differently, it would or could ruin their lives as though rape was somehow their fault. But, now...

now we are a society that supposedly talks about everything.

One article that came out not long after JJD was arrested had the title of the article go right to where my mind went. It was: Why did it take so long to arrest the Golden State Killer suspect? Interagency rivalries, old technology, errors and bad luck. Under that is a photograph of Larry Montgomery a retired investigator from Orange County. He said "Old technology, inter-agency rivalries and human error were all factors in the GSK decades long elusiveness. From the beginning it was thought by pretty much everyone who had experience chasing this perpetrator that he had military and or law enforcement experience.

I independently investigated this criminal over time spending three years intensely looking at who he could be as well as spent many years researching serial killers and their behaviors since the 1980 murders of Lyman and Charlene Smith who were members of our family. I too knew he was likely a cop. His arrogance is why I believed he was still in Sacramento as I have stated many times.

ARTICLE:

"In hindsight authorities say that DeAngelo fit their profile for the East Area Rapist also known as the Golden State Killer. Retired investigators have said "poor communication between agencies, investigative tunnel vision and antiquated technology all contributed to the Golden State

Killer's elusiveness." One investigator said simply "He was lucky" In 1975 and 76 detectives in the town of Visalia reached out to Sacramento Sheriffs. Apparently no one was interested in what they had according to Richard Shelby a retired detective who worked on these cases with Carol Daly. According to this article another reason given for the insularity between departments at the time was because of the theory the attacker may be a cop. One comment about this was "We could not be sure about the guy volunteering from the neighboring agencies. So what I derive from this comment is they are saying they did not speak to one another because of concern that the guy could be in one of their departments. This to me means they were afraid of red flagging the guy. Maybe understandable at the time, but 10 years later? Or 20? Or 30? If the trail led to a cop shop way back then, and there were notes in files and in jurisdictions about who they thought this guy was why no communication about it after the dust settled?

A regional task force was formed eventually including Sacramento County Sheriffs and city police, along with investigators from Davis and Contra Costa County. They say that new members were given blood tests to ensure they were not the rapist. Again, their caution was understandable in 1976-1979. DeAngelo **was** in another jurisdiction 20 minutes away. The article states that when DeAngelo was fired in Auburn for stealing the news of his termination never made it to the East Area Rapist task force. I find that difficult to believe all these years later and here is why. The crime of shoplifting by DeAngelo was committed in Sacramento County in their jurisdiction. They prosecuted him in Sacramento County. He was found guilty in Sacramento. I have to tilt my head slightly to the side here and have a ? planted on my forehead. I have a very hard time understanding and being able to believe that they had no idea that a fellow officer who was arrested in a store in their county not far from the attacks of the East Area Rapist was completely missed by the East Area Rapist task force? Now I am frowning. How does this happen? How did it happen? How was it allowed to stand for forty years? The store off Greenback truly WAS in their jurisdiction and truly was where EAR attacked. More ??????? So here is the rest of the article:

"The rapist's attacks around Sacramento had stopped months earlier, after Brian and Kate Maggiore were gunned down in Rancho Cordova in the killer's first documented slayings, so a petty theft elsewhere may not have been a red flag as much as it seemed in hindsight," Shelby said.

When the crimes shifted south, law enforcement there too approached the investigation in a vacuum. Between the end of 1979 and summer of 1981, DeAngelo is suspected of killing nine people in Southern California, starting in present-day Goleta with the slaying of Robert Offerman and Debra Manning, who were discovered bound in Offerman's bedroom.

Santa Barbara County Sheriff's Det. Fred Ray was assigned to the case but struggled to solve it without conclusive evidence. Then Lyman and Charlene Smith were killed in their bedroom in Ventura. The perpetrator had tied them up with a drapery cord. The day after the Smiths were killed, Ray said, he went to the scene and talked to the detectives. He told them that there had been a similar killing in Santa Barbara County and that he suspected the two crimes could be related.

The detectives didn't accept the premise and moved on with their own inquiry. Hampering investigators was the fact the Golden State Killer's crimes shared some similarities but were not identical in execution. Offerman and Manning were tied up and so were the Smiths — but they were killed with different weapons and bound with different types of knots, leading investigators to conclude they were unrelated. The Goleta killings of Offerman and Manning and Cheri Domingo and Gregory Sanchez targeted unmarried couples, steering investigators toward the belief the killer was driven by a moralistic ethos.

As authorities struggled to grasp the evolution of the Golden State Killer's attacks and the range of his geography, other crime sprees and misguided hunches sapped resources.

While DeAngelo was allegedly terrorizing Sacramento County as the East Area Rapist, several other serial rapists were operating in the area, Shelby said. There was the Vampire of Sacramento, who killed, cannibalized and drank the blood of some of his six victims and the Bedroom Basher, who raped and bludgeoned five women to death in Orange County.

Ray, the Santa Barbara County detective, said Ventura detectives brushed off his serial killer hunch because they already had a suspect in mind for the Smith killings.

Because the Smiths' heads were bashed in with a fireplace log in the middle of the night, investigators assumed from the brutish, up-close nature of the crime that the killer must have been someone close to the couple. Two years later, police arrested Lyman Smith's former business partner. He was ultimately freed after biological testing revealed a lack of evidence.

A similar misstep set back investigators in Orange County, where despite seeing some Golden State Killer hallmarks in the 1986 rape and slaying of Janelle Cruz in Irvine, authorities arrested the wrong man.

The case was worked by Larry Montgomery, who five years earlier as a new investigator in the Orange County Sheriff's Department had done the "gopher stuff" for the killing of Manuela Witthuhn, also in Irvine. DeAngelo is accused in that slaying, too.
In both cases, the women were raped and beaten to death."

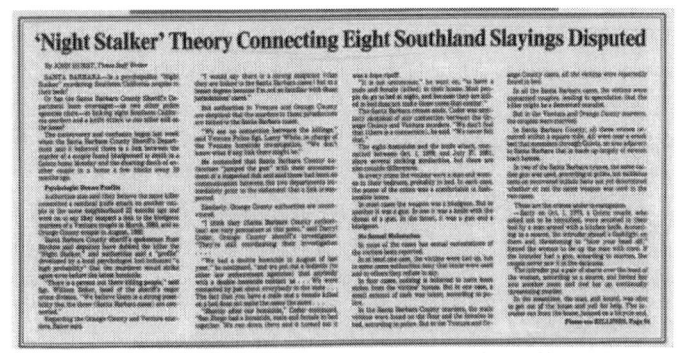

> **'Night Stalker' Theory Connecting Eight Southland Slayings Disputed**

A 1981 Los Angeles Times story described how different law enforcement agencies were in disagreement over whether several killings across the state were linked (Los Angeles Times)

Despite the parallels, Montgomery could not link the slayings, he said, because Gregory Gonzalez, who met Cruz in drug rehabilitation class, had confessed to an informant to her killing. In the time between Cruz's death and when her body was found, Gonzalez had been arrested on suspicion of a separate attempted rape.

"I wasn't looking for another suspect because it appeared to me to be Greg Gonzalez," Montgomery said. "Therefore there was nothing else to look for. I had a pretty darn good suspect. How often do they confess to it and attempt to do a similar crime two days before?"

Nearly a year after Cruz's death, Orange County prosecutors dropped the charges against Gonzalez despite his confession. Just like the previous case, blood and semen tests revealed he wasn't the attacker.

After the release, Montgomery continued to look for new evidence but struggled to scrounge up new leads.

"I was not thinking: This is a serial killer," he said.

The Smith and Cruz killings may not be the only ones where men were arrested for crimes allegedly committed by DeAngelo. Police in Simi Valley announced they are reviewing the slayings of Rhonda Wicht, 24, who was found beaten, raped and strangled, and her 4-year-old son, Donald, who was smothered in his bed, for any potential links.

A man who had been imprisoned for 39 years, Craig Coley, 70, was recently declared factually innocent of those killings and released and awarded $1.95 million for his time in custody.

Fred Ray, a retired Santa Barbara Sheriff's department investigator, worked the Golden State Killer case. (TOMAS OVALLE / Tomas Ovalle)

Much of the struggle to track the Golden State Killer and link him to the more than 100 burglaries, 46 rapes and dozen murders boils down to the technology and tactics of the time.

Police dogs were more frequently trained to sniff out drugs or explosives than they were people in the 1970s, which is how Phillips believes DeAngelo managed to elude capture.

During one manhunt, authorities had set up a perimeter that they believed trapped their suspect. After he wasn't found and the perimeter folded, detectives combing the area saw that someone had dug a shallow pit under a thick bush and apparently covered themselves with leaves to avoid detection. In another close call, the Visalia Ransacker shot his way out of a backyard and escaped in the night.

Staples of modern investigative work weren't available at the time. Cellphones weren't around to help authorities retrace a suspect's location through GPS. Home security cameras that would capture a prowler's image weren't as prevalent. Forensic science was still evolving. Crime scene analysis could pull a blood type or determine whether someone was not a "secretor" — an unusual genetic trait of not secreting blood type in saliva — but little more was available. Authorities mapped the crimes with corkboards and pins. They relied on guesswork, the occasional stakeout and in one case a trip inside the trunk of a potential victim's vehicle.

At the peak of the East Area Rapist's rampage, Phillips folded himself into a woman's trunk with her permission, then rode inside to her home. He didn't emerge until the garage doors were closed in case anyone was watching. The woman's profile and where she lived fit with the other attacks.

By nightfall, with black grease paint smeared on his face and skin, he set himself up at the end of the hallway steps from the woman's bedroom, facing the window through which the rapist was most likely to enter if he attacked that night. Then he waited. "If he came in that window, he wasn't going back out," Phillips said. But the suspect never appeared. "If we had the kind of crime pattern analysis that they have today, I think there was a good chance we would've caught him," he said.

Even pulling fingerprints off a victim's body through a method called iodine fuming was relatively new. And in many of the crimes, officials say DeAngelo used gloves. "In those days we didn't have DNA, "said Ray, the former Santa Barbara County detective. "Other than ballistics we had very little evidence from the scene that would connect all the cases."

In Orange County, Ronald Veach, who led the investigation of the Witthuhn case, tried to connect the Irvine and Santa Barbara County killings and the slayings of Keith and Patrice Harrington in Dana Point by focusing on ligatures. But a test of the fibers used to tie up victims in each case was a dead end, he said.

"There wasn't a week that went by where I didn't think about the case and things I may have missed or didn't see and it went well on into my retirement," he said. "We couldn't say definitively that any cases were tied because we didn't have the DNA at the time to do it. But based on M.O. we felt there were many similarities."

The multiple investigations that failed to identify DeAngelo as a suspect were victims of their time, said Ron Martinelli, a retired San Jose police detective and expert forensic criminologist who was never involved in investigating the Golden State Killer.

"We had no patterning, criminal psychological profiling" or strict protocols for maintaining the integrity of a crime scene, he said. "It was just basically a lot of gumshoe and asking questions and trying to gather as much evidence as possible."

DNA technology fully arrived in 2000, and relative to the decades before, the investigation into the Golden State Killer began evolving much more rapidly. At first came a wave of media coverage announcing that the man who had prowled Visalia was also the man who raped in Sacramento and killed there and in Southern California. His moniker graduated to the Golden State Killer, triggering a wave of national headlines, exposes on true-crime TV and theories about his identity.

Many of the detectives who had been tracking the crimes in isolation over the decades kept tabs on the investigation. Some continued working the case after their retirements.

Investigators regularly searched the usual databases for DNA matches including with the FBI and Interpol, without success. Only recently did they tap into the world of genealogy and family history.

This year, Paul Holes, a Contra Costa County district attorney investigator approaching retirement, compared crime scene DNA with a genealogy website full of family histories and hereditary information. Within weeks, authorities were surveilling DeAngelo in Citrus Heights, a Sacramento suburb.

In the six days before his arrest April 24, detectives surreptitiously obtained two samples of DeAngelo's discarded DNA.

It was the match they had been waiting for, prosecutors say."
**4:35 p.m.:** This article was updated to clarify the definition of a secretor.
**10:20 a.m.:** This article was updated with additional details from a detective.
*This article was originally published at 3 a.m.*

*Article by Joseph Serna and Benjamin Oreskes from the LA Times May 25, 2018*

Joseph Serna is a Metro reporter who has been with the Los Angeles Times since 2012. He previously worked for papers in Orange County and Signal Hill, a 2.2-square-mile city surrounded by Long Beach. He was part of the team that won the Pulitzer Prize for Breaking News for coverage of the 2015 San Bernardino terrorist attack and is a graduate of California's community college and Cal State systems.

Footnote regarding the investigations comment by Ron Martinelli in this article. Mr. Martinelli mentions they failed to identify a suspect and that they were victims of their time. I agree completely with that statement. All of the jurisdictions and all of the investigators of their time did they best they could with the technology, the funding and the restrictions placed on them by all of those things as well as the agencies and the people they worked for. When a task force was formed in any jurisdiction to try and find the guy responsible for so much carnage after a time those task forces had to be disbanded. Economics played a part in this story overall along with so many other limitations of their time.

Regarding the comments about ballistics by former Santa Barbara County detective Fred Ray, he states "Other than ballistics we had very little evidence from the scene that would connect all the cases."

**My comment is**: were the ballistics something that would have or did tell your department at the time that what was used would definitively tell all of you that you were looking for law enforcement?

**In addition there is an error in the paragraph about the Lyman and Charlene Smith murders. The business associate was not cleared by any form of biological testing at the time he was released from jail. That did not occur until years later. My comments:

*And then an additional footnote from Anne: Regarding the arrest and freedom of a suspect in 1981-82 for the Smith murders there is more to the story. A business associate of Lyman Smith's was arrested on the word of a pastor. The pastor who had counseled the business associate who initials are JA. The pastor said JA had confessed to the crimes. There was no biological evidence it is true, but they did not know that at the time. No evidence linked the business associate with the murders except what was the word of a Pastor who as they investigated turned out to not only be a liar, but someone who had inserted himself into another case in the past as he tried to be "helpful." There*

210

was a fingerprint on a wine glass left the night before the murders when the business associate admitted he had stopped by for a visit on March 12, 1980. After arresting a business associate who had absolutely nothing to do with the murders in 1981, and after having him sit in jail for a year it was determined by Ventura County prosecutors that there was no evidence to try the case as their star witnesses was determined to be unreliable. The charges were finally dropped. I have not mentioned the business associates name only his initials, as he paid enough over time for a crime he did not commit. The charges were dismissed and he was freed in 1982. But, then the case went cold. Eventually Ventura was also to eliminate JA as a POI because they tested his DNA.

In addition, my comments are that this article really does cover very well the many reasons EAR, ONS, GSK was allowed his freedom all of these years. In retrospect it is unfortunate as many man and woman hours were dedicated to trying to find the perpetrator in each department and in each jurisdiction After the crimes appeared to cease as far as we know to date, the long periods of time, sometimes years would go by with no cold case unit that worked the cases in different departments.

In the winter of 2016 for example I spoke to a homicide detective in Ventura County. I asked about the case and identified why I was asking. I told him who I was. I asked him if they had a cold case unit working on the murders. His response was no they did not, but they would follow any leads that might come in. He asked me "What is it you *want?" I said details, information, a police report of the response the day of the murders. A report. Of course I was told that a case number did not exist because there was no suspect and no arrest so no case number, only a report number.*

*I contacted the Medical Examiners Office to see if they could help me with anything after almost forty years. They tried to be helpful, but at first and for the next two weeks they could not locate the files with the medical examiners reports on the Smith murders. It was 2016. They did call and tell me the records had been found, but LE did not want anything released as this was still an open murder investigation. Protocol.*

## More sightings and more crimes

### In Brief — 12/12/77

**Masked Bike Rider Eludes Police**

A bicycle-riding man wearing a ski mask eluded police in the East Area early Sunday.

First spotted by sheriff's deputies on the Watt Avenue bridge at 2:30 a.m., the bike rider was wearing a ski hood which covered his head and had an opening for his face. Deputies lost sight of the man but he reportedly was spotted again two hours later by city patrolmen near an apartment complex on La Riviera Drive near Watt.

He left the bicycle there. Officers said it was listed as stolen in Redding.

The East Area rapist, who reportedly wears a mask during his attacks, has struck three times in the area of La Riviera Drive and Watt. However, officers said later Sunday that the bike rider probably was not the rapist.

Opportunity Lost

**December 12, 1977** – then there is this small article – sounded like it was him, looked like it was him – why were the sheriff's deputies not able to stop this guy and at least question him? The last line of the article makes me just shake my head because this could have been the end of the East Area Rapists reign of terror.

**In Brief – Masked Bike Rider Eludes Police ARTICLE**

A bicycle riding man wearing a ski mask eluded police in the East area early Sunday.

First spotted by sheriff's deputies on the Watt Avenue Bridge at 2:30 a.m. the bike rider was wearing a ski hood which covered his head and had an opening for his face. Deputies lost sight of the man but he reportedly was spotted again two hours later by city patrolmen near an apartment complex on La Riviera Drive near Watt.

He left the bicycle there. Officers said it was listed as stolen in Redding.

The East Area rapist, who reportedly wears a mask during his attacks, has struck three times in the area of La Riviera Drive and Watt. However, officers said later Sunday that the bike rider **probably was not the rapist. END OF ARTICLE**

My opinion and possibly many others would think that it PROBABLY WAS the rapist. He had the advantage. He was on a bike; they were in a car. Very smart.

## ADDITIONAL REASONS RAPISTS AND OTHER CRIMINALS ARE NOT CAUGHT

Crime labs have grappled with limited capacity and state and local law enforcement budgets have tightened, untested kits have piled up across the country.

- **Crime lab resources.** While public crime labs throughout the country have struggled to maintain sufficient funding and personnel in recent years, technology has advanced and the demand for DNA testing has grown dramatically. In addition to rape kit evidence, crime labs receive DNA samples from hundreds and in many cases, thousands of crime scenes each year. The result has been exceedingly long turn-around times—sometimes years—for testing.
- **Police resources.** Many kits never make it to a crime lab in the first place and instead spend years—even decades—sitting untested in police storage facilities. Law enforcement agencies often lack the technology to track untested rape kits and the personnel needed for shipping or transporting untested kits to a crime lab in a timely manner. These agencies further lack resources and staffing to investigate and follow up on leads resulting from rape kit testing.

Another reason behind the backlog is **detective discretion**. In the majority of jurisdictions, the decision whether to send a rape kit for testing rests solely within the discretion of the officer assigned to the case. Several factors can affect the officer's decision, including:

- **Whether the department prioritizes sexual assaults.** Law enforcement agencies often fail to dedicate the time and resources that other crimes receive to sexual assault cases. More than with any other crime, members of law enforcement frequently disbelieve or even blame victims of sexual assault rather than focusing on bringing the perpetrator to justice.
- **Whether the case is likely to move forward.** Due to a lack of understanding about how trauma can affect a survivor of rape, officers often misinterpret survivors' reactions and choices in the immediate aftermath of the assault as being "uncooperative" or "not credible." In addition to the biological and emotional impact of recovering from the direct trauma, survivors also may be hesitant to participate in the criminal justice process for a number of reasons, including fear of retaliation, being treated poorly by members of law enforcement, shame and not wanting others, such as family and friends, to know about the assault.
- 
- **Whether the identity of the perpetrator is known.** Many jurisdictions only test kits in cases where the assailant is unknown in order to attempt to identify a suspect through DNA evidence. It is important to remember, however, that rape kit testing has significant

value beyond identifying an unknown suspect, including the ability to confirm a suspect's contact with a victim, corroborate the victim's account of the attack, link unsolved crimes to a serial offender and exonerate innocent suspects. Testing every rape kit booked into evidence ensures greater access to justice for survivors and signals to perpetrators that they will be held accountable for their crimes.

Jurisdictions that are deeply invested in bringing justice to survivors and preventing future crimes have dedicated the necessary resources toward addressing their backlogs and moving cases forward. New York City served as a model for the rest of the country when it committed to testing every rape kit in its backlog and aggressively following up on leads and prosecuting cases. Detroit is now working to pull together the resources needed to test every kit in its backlog of more than 11,000 untested kits and to investigate the resulting leads. In Cleveland prosecutors have initiated cases against hundreds of perpetrators as testing has begun on a backlog of nearly 4,000 kits. And in Memphis nearly 6,000 kits have already been tested as the Memphis Police Department addresses their backlog of 12,164 kits. http://www.endthebacklog.org/backlog/why-backlog-exists **END OF ARTICLE**

## Chapter Nine

## Larry Crompton

## Written by Larry Crompton

April 24th, 2018, with the arrest of Joseph James DeAngelo, many victims and families began to have a feeling of closure for the many rapes and murders committed by this violent sex offender. Many officers and civilians who worked on the cases over the forty-two years it took to finally close the cases also felt a feeling of thankfulness.

Although the arrest was made it also was a lesson that law enforcement must learn from. It does no good to live in the past but it proves to all that we must learn from the past. What did detectives miss when the crimes were occurring? What was the thoughts on certain crimes back in the seventies? What were the thoughts on rapes and the victims? Many rapes were ignored because the victim did not know the rapist. Many times they were not looked upon as a serious crime as the victim was not hurt. At times it was looked upon as the victim was to blame. or at least partly to blame. Many of DeAngelo's victims were teenagers, two were only thirteen yet cooperation between agencies was not a priority. Many times if you were not in the area where the crimes happened, other agencies did not know of the crimes. Many times the crimes were not reported to the news media as it was felt that the perpetrator would learn that he was being looked for and would be more cautious.

What we must learn from the past is that cooperation is needed by all agencies and that civilians can and do play an important part in solving crimes. In many cases detectives did not see the terror that was in the minds of the victims. That was not the case in DeAngelo's victims. They all knew that they were going to die because of the terror he put in their minds and many victims knew that the rape was not the worst that could happen. It only took a few attacks before law enforcement began to realize the danger that was happening in their areas and the fear that was so strong in the minds of those trying to deal with fear.

DeAngelo was not the most active rapist in the 70's but he was the most violent of any in California's history. Detectives working the cases knew from his actions that he wanted to kill. A Doctor working with incarcerated rapists who I contacted learned from her rapists that they knew he wanted to kill and was not just a rapist needing sex. Sex was not his priority the Doctor said and when he found the justification to kill he would. She and other Psychologists felt that the rapist would not be taken alive. He would kill the officer trying to arrest him or he would kill himself. This was a proven fact over the years of DeAngelo's attacks. Years later it was learned that murders and the shooting of a young boy chasing him was because of that sick mind.

DeAngelo did not talk to his victims about the sex he was after and how beautiful or sexy they were and this was totally alien from any rape crimes that they had heard of. Sex was not his motivation and because of that he was more cold and unfeeling than any before or after him. Because of that detectives soon learned that he was a dangerous and deadly attacker.

Many detectives and civilians donated their career and times to try and identify this rapist and murderer. It was their dedication that kept the investigation going over the years. Many crimes are simply considered "cold cases" and filed away. Sometimes because of lack of employees cases are left uninvestigated.

During my career I was involved in many investigations and felt that it was my responsibility to solve the crimes. Fortunately, many were solved although two remained on my mind for many years because I could not find closure. One was a young thirteen-year-old girl who was kidnapped, raped and murdered. Three years after I retired I got a subpoena to testify in court. The rapist/kidnapper/murderer was convicted and sent to prison. The other case was a rapist/kidnapper/murderer named Joseph James DeAngelo who was arrested April twenty-fifth, twenty eighteen. Both of these were closures for families and victims of crimes committed by the worst of the worst. After the arrest and conviction of the rapist/murderer of the teenager, my mind went into another direction. For many years I was afraid that EAR/ONS would go free. Now I had the feeling that there was a chance that he would be found.

When I was working the cases I learned how sadistic EAR was. I went over all the previous cases and because of his knowledge about guns I felt he was a military person or had family members who were. Also the possibility of law enforcement connections had been talked about yet connections were not found. I am sure many detectives hoped and prayed it would not be law enforcement yet when DeAngelo was arrested and his six years of law enforcement proven, no one had any regrets. Prayers were from all that closure was there and the victims and family could now at least find some satisfaction.

I was a deputy working in the Crime Lab helping the criminalists process scenes when I first learned of the East Area Rapist. Although thirty-six attacks by the rapist and possibly two murders and the shooting of a teenager had happened we knew nothing about the rapist or his crimes. We were only an hour's drive from the Sacramento crimes and minutes from some of the other rapes yet we knew nothing until Lt. Root and Sgt. Bevin's from the Sacramento East Area Rapist Task Force came to Contra Costa to tell us that they thought that EAR was heading in our direction. They told us how violent he was and that our agencies needed to form a Task Force to work the cases. Unfortunately, in those times agencies did not work together and needed information was not always passed on.

The Sacramento Task Force detectives were very helpful in our investigations. They kept nothing to themselves as they knew how violent the East Area Rapist was and that the victims needed closure. Their main concern was to prevent any more victims from coming under the violence and threats. The fear that he put into the minds of the victims also entered the minds of the detectives. It was that fear that kept the investigations going by the Sacramento Task Force and the Contra Costa Task Force. Other agencies where victims were attacked did what they could to help however when only one or two attacks happened they were not completely involved.

In talking to many victims I learned of their feelings, the fear, the terror and in the male's mind the thought that they did not protect their wife or their partner. I tried to tell them that had they fought, had they tried to stop the rapist they would have cost the lives of them and their loved ones. Fortunately, some were able to live with that thought, others couldn't and divorces happened.

The cases I worked, that I was involved in, never left my mind. I could not lose the feeling that I had not completed my job. I did not catch this violent rapist. Six of the first ten attacks were teenagers. The youngest two were fifteen. In all the attacks in Northern California, fourteen were teenagers, two were thirteen. This cemented in my mind as these young girls proved to me that sex was not DeAngelo's reason for the attacks. It was his deranged mind and the terror he wanted to put in the victims' minds and all others in the areas he attacked. His last known attack was also a teenager. He murdered young Janelle Cruz, a beautiful young lady who had a life to look forward to, until DeAngelo ended it.

I did not know of Janelle's murder at the time. Sgt. Bevin's and I heard of the murder of Robert Offerman and Debra Manning and we felt in our hearts that the murderer was our rapist but we got no cooperation. Soon I learned of a couple who were able to get away from a rapist. Again Sgt. Bevin's and I went over the reports and again we were convinced, but again we were alone in our thoughts. I heard of other murders in Southern California yet still no cooperation.

It was not until April 2000 when I got a call from Criminalist Paul Holes telling me he was a DNA expert and if I could give him names of victims in my area he would do the DNA match. I gave him three names and three months later he called me and told me that the match was made. I told him that I knew of five murders in Southern California and if he could get a Criminalist to cooperate I knew that their murderer was our rapist. Seven months later he called me and said that they had ten murders and they had joined six of them with our EAST AREA RAPIST. I was flown to Orange County to talk to their Original Night Stalker Task Force. I met with Sgt. Larry Pool, a very dedicated officer working the murders. I gave him the reports of all the Northern

California attacks so he could see what violent type attacker he was looking for.

I learned of the Dec. 30, 1979 murders of Robert Offerman and Debra Manning, the March 30, 1980 murders of Lyman and Charlene Smith, August 19, 1980 murders of Keith and Patrice Harrington, the Feb, 6, 1981 murder of Manuela Witthuhn, the July 27, 1981 murders of Greg Sanchez and Cheri Domingo and the May 4, 1986 murder of the young teenager Janelle Cruz.

Although the statute of limitations had run out on our violent rapes in Northern California, I knew now that because of the dedication I saw in Sgt Pool, the investigation and the possibility of closure for all the victims and families could happen.

Looking back, I now know that cooperation between agencies must occur to find closure in all crimes and after the arrest of DeAngelo, it confirms in my mind that crimes cannot be closed without the dedication of civilians who also are determined for closure.

When I got involved in the cases in 1978 and saw the fear in the minds of the victims I could not let it go. I couldn't sleep at night knowing that EAR was out roaming the areas to get ready to attack again. My mind wrapped around what I would do if my family was part of these horrible crimes. As a law enforcement officer I knew I had to look at it differently, but as a victim as these were I don't know if I could have handled it that way. It was because of these thoughts and feelings that I knew I could never give up on trying to have these crimes solved. After

I retired I was fortunate to be in contact with those who were as dedicated as I was in finding closure for the victims and families. They never gave up and now I can believe that other cold case crimes will be solved.

## Chapter Ten

## Mark Smith

### A Question of Ballistics

I first became aware of this case EARONS in the early 2000s from watching the original Cold Case Files with Bill Kurtis, and being a fellow human being I was aghast and sickened by it. I would periodically over the years check on the internet to see if the case had progressed any, figuring authorities were actively investigating it, and had his DNA. I was surprised that after many years EARONS was still unidentified.

In the original story on Cold Case Files when talking of the EAR end of the case, it was stated early on the perpetrator could be a cop. I had doubts at the time that he was LE, due to my belief a cop wouldn't do such heinous acts, and his personality would prevent him functioning as a police officer, which I suspect many people felt.

Originally reading online, following along with many opinions about what type of person he was and often with the theories about his employment such as a trades person, in construction, possibly in real estate, a delivery driver etc., I tended to agree with this line of reasoning, without giving it much critical thought myself.

He was very tactical, I felt was a very experienced criminal, likely 25 to 30 years of age, possibly in a position or had ties in such a way that would allow him to be above suspicion, but not a police officer. I was wrong and in 2016 my belief would begin to change.

In the spring of 2016 I decided to really look at the case more in-depth, studying the details, as well as joining the Pro Board dedicated to the case. The tactics were far greater than I had given him credit for. He was not lucky dozens to a hundred or more times, he was far too capable of eluding law enforcement , this man was trained, police and/or military. On the Pro Board, some members felt this way as well, and with this in mind further persuaded me to think he likely was a cop/military during his time as EAR. I would shortly thereafterbegin to lean towards him being police due to what I saw as someone who likely knew police procedures, timing, and as Richard Shelby noted that he could be listening in.

This would also explain if he too was the Visalia Ransacker. The dysfunction that I thought originally would prevent him from being a cop would not come to the surface fully until 1979 when he was fired for theft, so he could have been a cop for a time, likely until he moved south. At this point could his firing have been the tipping point for his transition to murder?

The physical evidence that clinched it for me, if accurate, was the use of 110 grain Super Vel ammunition used at the Offerman/Manning murder scene. At the time such ammunition was only available to LE/Security officers. Essentially that ammunition was designed to boost the energy of 38 Special revolvers, which conventionally used most often 158 grain bullets at much lower velocities. The lighter weight of the 110 grain bullets would increase muzzle velocity and energy levels similar to a 9mm. Now with that, I also began to question Law Enforcement in Santa Barbara regarding this ballistics evidence, that if true, did they not look into this? The ballistic evidence at the Domingo/Sanchez scene, what was that? Was there a possible connection there? Was it possibly the same gun and/or ammunition? Comments from an article May 2018 by former Santa Barbara County detective Fred Ray, he states "Other than ballistics we had very little evidence from the scene that would connect all the cases."

Another question I have regarding ballistics is the Maggiore attack, that in June 2016 Sacramento LE determined that the 1978 killings was perpetrated by EAR, and if that is correct, how is it that the caliber is undetermined in that circumstance? Did they not recover bullets? Were the bullets too badly damaged? Did the bullets not leave definitive holes in clothing, or tissue? I began to wonder could the ballistics possibly connect to Santa Barbara? Could the bullets be 110 grain Super Vel?

I was introduced to Anne Penn's book in January 2017 through a Facebook posting forwarded to me by a fellow proboarder. After a read through of her book, what struck me was that she believed that EAR lived outside the most common attack zones. It was because of this more unconventional theory I made a friend request on Facebook to her. After a time, she confided in me that she felt EARONS was a cop, as I was inclined to believe as well, and he still lived in Sacramento.

Her belief that during the EAR period he lived outside the attack area including outside the county, she had begun looking into smaller towns around Sacramento. I was very intrigued by Anne Penn's overall theory, which included a specific suspect, based on someone she had gone to high school with was quite close to what EARONS would be shown to be in Joseph James Deangelo, and she was definitely on the right track. Do I think she would have solved it? I don't know, but if there was a lay person who might have solved it, I wouldn't have been surprised if she did.

I am relieved for Anne and her family, as well as all victims, survivors, and their families that at long last there's a suspect in custody. I hope that he lives to see the day that the foreman says guilty.

I would like to express my admiration to those police officers, those on the ground doing the work. I have no doubt there were many dedicated officers trying their best to solve it, but weren't given the resources to adequately pursue it at the time and continue on with it over the years.

My directive now is to ask questions of those jurisdictional heads who would oversee the investigations, the management so to speak.

Cold Case Files stated early on he could be a cop, who stated that to the show? Law Enforcement? What happened with that?

Why wasn't there cooperation among jurisdictions? Why did it take over 40 years to identify him? Was there not an ongoing investigation?

Why did it take until January 2018 for the authorities to look at public genealogy websites, which I thought they had been doing all along? I was wrong, it wasn't active for decades.

He was a successful predator because he was a cop.

He attacked dozens of people, killed at least 13, why was there no large scale task force put together over the decades? Where were the state authorities on this? This case could have and should have been solved long ago, decades ago. I would like to see these questions asked and answered truthfully.

Finally, I would like to see an end of Misogyny. Sexual assault, along with other violence exists at a level of some 90 to 95 percent perpetrated by men. This is wrong, and always has been throughout history. In the current political and social environment, the MeToo movement expresses that it continues despite it being 2018. We have a long way to go. I have no doubt that the EAR attacks, particularly early on were not given the attention that they deserved as rape was not considered by society as a major crime, this no doubt aided the criminal. I hope it doesn't take another 42 years to change our serious lack of progress here.

DeAngelo's home in Citrus Heights collecting any possible evidence

Second updated booking sheet with charges

April 25, 2018 booked into custody 2:29 a.m.

| |
|---|
| VENTURA COUNTY SHERIFF'S DEPARTMENT (Case# 1161124)<br>Felony | Bail:No Bail |
| SANTA BARBARA COUNTY SHERIFF'S DEPARTMENT (Case# WR018095)<br>Felony | Bail:No Bail |
| ORANGE COUNTY SHERIFF'S DEPARTMENT (Case# 18HF0599)<br>Felony | Bail:No Bail |
| ORANGE COUNTY SHERIFF'S DEPARTMENT (Case# 18HF0599)<br>Felony | Bail:No Bail |

Additional Charges are Kidnapping for Ransom or to commit extortion or robbery PC 209(B) Felony Kidnapping for robbery

EAST AREA RAPIST ARRESTED If you have been following the news, you know the person accused of being the East Area Rapist (also known as the Original Night Stalker and the Golden State Killer) was arrested on April 24 by detectives from the Sacramento County Sheriff's Department. 72-Year-old Joseph James DeAngelo of Citrus Heights was taken into custody without incident based upon DNA linking him as a positive match for the DNA profile of the perpetrator who terrorized our area during 1977-78--and later expanded to other locations throughout California. He is being held in Sacramento County Jail without bail. The arrest was the result of a renewed effort led by Sacramento County District Anne Marie Schubert to review the multiple cases over forty years old.

Through the hard work of investigators meticulously processing evidence, conducting interviews, and gathering new information, the arrest was made to make sure justice is served for the victims and family's connected to these cases from their respective jurisdictions.

A press conference was held following the arrest that included DA Schubert and Sacramento County Sheriff Scott Jones

## Chapter Eleven

## In the beginning – What made DeAngelo so evil?

Where do we begin with JJD aka Creep? There is so much we already know based on what the media has reported, what sleuth sites say from public record. In my previous books I have profiled the killer and so I will restate here that I do not believe this man just happened upon this type of life and these types of crimes. I think JJD knew very early on that he was different and so he planned to grow into and become what he saw as his career path. He wanted to learn to become great at prowling, stalking, burglary and rape. He was patient as he began because he knew that eventually his path would lead him to rape and then after that rape and murder. It was intentional, planned, studied and practiced.

He wanted to be in charge and have power and control. Early on he killed animals, and in particular the creep hated dogs. Likely they were the first creature to die at the hands of JJD as early as from the age of 10-12. This man planned to become a cop. What better way to learn Law Enforcement methods and use this career in which to hide, in which to learn how to avoid capture?

There is always much debate and discussion as to why and how a man or person learns or decides to take a human life, but in these cases that was not enough. JJD wanted to terrify and control everyone. He was successful at this endeavor. JJD became a sexual terrorist of the first kind. He likely would have had anger issues, rages and rants taking things out on those closest to him just based on his own physiology as well as his psychology. The nature versus nurture debate in JJD's case would be that this man was doomed from the beginning. It takes an interesting combination of the perfect storm of conditions to evolve into a terrorist such as this.

I would be willing to bet if one were to perform a brain scan on JJD they would likely find some differences or abnormality in his amygdala and possibly a scan would show some differences in certain areas of the brain that not only control self-control (the prefrontal cortex), but his scans would show more information about the issues involved in what makes a serial killer in a biological sense. Then, there is actual brain chemistry involved and again I would be willing to bet that JJD is lacking in certain brain chemicals that have to do with endorphins and melatonin.

The levels of chemicals needed in order to sleep, in order to find self-control as well as the chemicals that happen that feed into rage reactions, adrenaline and other chemicals in his chemistry set were off. Then add to that his nurture which encapsulated childhood trauma and abuse. You have an individual that by the age of 10 is anti-social personality already. The environment JJD grew up in at the hands of his parents and in particular his father, the rage involved with the feelings of having no control there are huge. JJD then apparently was traumatized as a ten-year-old as he watched or witnessed the rape of his sister by two men. He had extremely conflicted feelings about it and had NO ONE to talk to about it. He internalized the experience which was confusing at the very least. The images stayed in his mind. He likely had mixed emotions about something that was scary, traumatizing and confusing as well as sexually stimulating to contend with, again with no help from adults. It could be that if this story of the rapes is true that young Joseph and his sister never told a soul. These things were not discussed especially in the 1950's. An article recently written on Buzz Fed News by Stephanie K. Bauer in May 2018 tells us that these issues among family members were also true and written about in my first two books about the cases. I have taken bits and pieces from it following:

**The Suspected Golden State Killer Witnessed Two Men Rape His Sister. It May Have Fueled His Rampage.**

"Maybe that was the start of Joe going wacko," said a nephew of Joseph DeAngelo, the man suspected of being the prolific killer".

"Decades before he killed at least 12 people and sexually assaulted 51 others in a prolific crime spree that terrorized the state of California, the suspected Golden State Killer watched two men rape his younger sister on an Air Force base in Germany, family members said.

## The CREEP Among Us * Anne Penn

Joseph James DeAngelo, 72, who was identified last month as the serial rapist and killer who terrorized California in the 1970s and 1980s, was playing with his sister Constance in an abandoned warehouse on the base when two airmen walked in and raped her in front of him, Jesse Ryland, one of Constance's sons, told BuzzFeed News this week.

DeAngelo was about 9 or 10 at the time. His sister was 7 years old.

Another part of the article from Buzz Feed:

His sister's rape was just one notable incident in what was a tough childhood for DeAngelo, his nephew said.

DeAngelo and his three siblings grew up in an abusive household where his father physically assaulted his mother, Kathleen, said Ryland. She also abused at least one of the children.

"She would hit my mom all the time," Ryland said, adding that his mother would at times wear two pairs of pants to lessen the blow. "I'm pretty positive they were all abused like that."

Ryland said when his uncle and his mother told their parents about what had happened in the military base warehouse, they were instructed to never discuss it.

Burgess said that might have been confusing for DeAngelo, and the conflict between his parents also could have affected his psychological state."

End of excerpts from the article. My comments:

So we see that there was a conspiracy of silence within the family to not talk about ANYTHING that was a conflict or issue. The siblings were instructed never to discuss the attack or rapes. They were left to try to cope with what it all meant and how they felt about it. Their father and mother were abusive according to relatives who were speaking out in the article shown.

## Chapter Twelve

## What we know about JJD so far

What do we know so far? As it turns out, quite a bit. Joseph James DeAngelo was born November 8, 1945 in Bath New York to his mother Kathleen Louise DeGroat and her husband Joseph DeAngelo Senior.

Joseph DeAngelo's mother was named Kathleen DeGroat DeAngelo and later took the name Kathleen Bosanko when she remarried. DeAngelo's biological father was named Joseph James DeAngelo Sr., and he hailed from Watkins Glen, New York. JJD's mother was a waitress at Denny's.

**Joseph DeAngelo's Father Was an Airman in World War II Who Died in South Korea**

According to an old newspaper article from 1944 in the Star-Gazette, the suspect's father, Sgt. Joseph DeAngelo, was awarded seven clusters to the Air Medal for meritorious achievement. His 15th Army Air Force unit holds a presidential citation for the "low level attack on the Ploesti oil fields in Romania," the old newspaper article states. "The top turret gunner received the decorations in a ceremony on an Italian airfield. He has flown in raids on targets in Italy, France, Austria and Germany."

DeAngelo's father, then of Bath, New York, was wounded in action over Australia. He was serving with the Army Air Force as a gunner

## Watkins Glen Flier Wins High Honors

S/Sgt. Joseph DeAngelo, son of Mrs. Mary F. DeAngelo of Watkins Glen who visited Elmira friends a few days ago has been awarded seven clusters to the Air Medal for meritorious achievement.

While here, Sgt. DeAngelo was reluctant to discuss his adventures over Europe, but it has been learned that his unit, **DeAngelo** the 15th Army Air Force, holds a Presidential citation for the low level attack on the Ploesti oil fields in Romania.

The top turret gunner received the decorations in a ceremony on an Italian airfield. He has flown in raids on targets in Italy, France, Austria and Germany.

His wife, Kathleen, lives in Bath.

on a B-24 bomber. He had entered the service in April 1942 and was trained at the Biloxi Air Base in Biloxi, Mississippi. He left the United States with a combat group in 1943, according to another archived news article.

This is the wedding announcement for the suspect's parents, who were married in a Baptist Church in 1941 in New York. His mother was the daughter of Mr. and Mrs. Charles DeGroat, and his father was the son of Mr. and Mrs. Samuel DeAngelo (His mother's name was Mary DeAngelo, and ancestral records show she was an Italian immigrant).

Kathleen DeGroat to Joseph DeAngelo Senior
November 20, 1941

## Miss DeGroat's Wedding Held

The marriage of Miss Kathleen DeGroat on Nov. 20, 1941, to Joseph DeAngelo, son of Mr. and Mrs. Samuel DeAngelo of Watkins Glen, is announced by her parents, Mr. and Mrs. Charles DeGroat, 613½ Lake St.

The Rev. Joseph D. McDanel of the Elmwood Ave. Baptist Church, Elmira Heights, performed the service in his parsonage. The couple will live in the Heights.

It's not clear when the suspect's parents split up. DeAngelo Jr. was born in November 1945. In 1949, his parents had another son, according to a newspaper birth announcement.

The obituary for Kathleen Louise Bosanko says she was 87 when she died in 2010 and left behind four children, one of whom was Joe DeAngelo. "She was a beautiful person and a wonderful Mother," the obituary says.

Her headstone refers to her as "Ramblin Rose," although it's not clear why. According to the Sacramento Bee, DeAngelo had a brother, and his mother worked as a waitress at Denny's. Her new husband, Jack Bosanko, served in the Navy in World War II, according to burial records. They married in Tulare, California. Bosanko was known as "Kay."

Burial records show that DeAngelo's father's brother was a World War II and Korean War veteran who is buried at Arlington National Cemetery and received the Purple Heart. An old newspaper article reported that the suspect's brother was injured in the Vietnam War and hospitalized in Guam. By that point, 1971, Kathleen was Kathleen Bosanko and living in Auburn, California, with her husband Jack. An artilleryman, DeAngelo Jr.'s brother lost a finger in the Vietnam conflict. After.graduating from Folsom High in 1964, DeAngelo Jr., the suspect, served in the Vietnam

War. An archived 1967 article from a California newspaper shows that Joseph J. DeAngelo Jr. served in the U.S. Navy as a damage control man 2nd class on the USS Canberra, which was "expected to dock at San Diego … following service on the gun line off North Vietnam." Another article reported that he completed basic training in December 1964

According to The Sacramento Bee, a former neighbor named Doug Burgarel said that DeAngelo moved to rural Auburn, California with his mother and stepfather when he was a teenager.

"DeAngelo's stepfather worked for Burgarel's father at Sierra Crane and Hoist as a welder making indoor overhead cranes," reported the newspaper.

His sister, Rebecca Thompson, told The Bee that she was shocked by his arrest, saying, "As stunned as I am – because I've never seen him display any kind of madness or anything like that – I just can't believe it. I've never seen anything to allow myself to think he could do such things."

## JJD was in the Navy

**JOSEPH J. DEANGELO**

Joseph J. DeAngelo, damage controlman 2nd class, serving aboard the USS Canberra, is expected to dock at San Diego today, following service on the gun line off North Vietnam.

The son of Mr. and Mrs. Jack Bosanko of Rt. 3, Box 3085, Auburn, the 21-year-old sailor is expected home on leave soon. The Canberra is returning via Formosa and Australia.

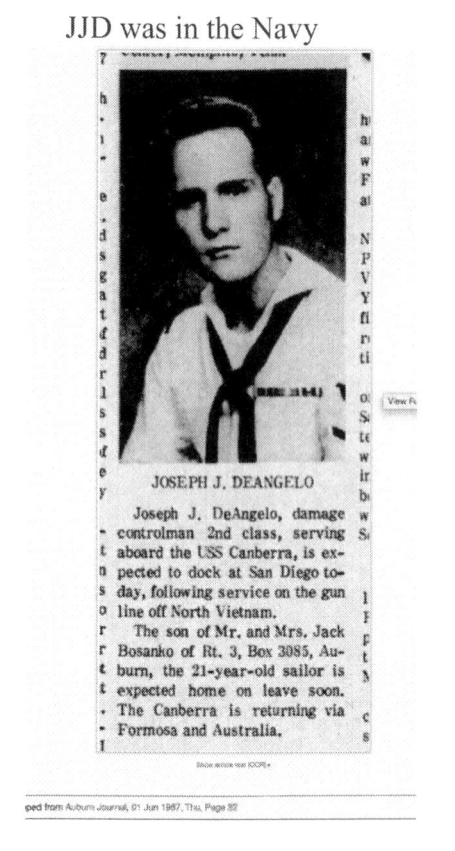

June 1, 1967 article above

Joseph J. DeAngelo, damage control man 2$^{nd}$ class, serving aboard the USS Canberra, is expected to dock at San Diego today, following service on the gun line off North Vietnam.

The son of Mr. and Mrs. Jack Bosanko of Rt. 3, Box 3085, Auburn, the 21-year-old sailor is expected home on leave soon. The Canberra is returning via Formosa and Australia. END OF ARTICLE

## The CREEP Among Us * Anne Penn

Sometime prior to 1972 Joseph DeAngelo met Bonnie Colwell. Since the two had gone to Sierra College as well as Cal State University in Sacramento they must have met and dated. They even got so far as to become engaged to one another. The announcement for that engagement was in the newspaper. The engagement was called off at some point by Bonnie as far as we can surmise to this point. Not too long after the break-up Bonnie dated and became engaged to another man who it was stated was from Sacramento. In the interest of their privacy, I will not rename him here – I am posting the article which is difficult to read when copied and reduced. In short Bonnie Colwell married another man in August 1972.

Bonnie (left) DeAngelo (right)

The CREEP Among Us * Anne Penn

Bonnie Jean Colwell

## Colwell - DeAngelo Pair Announce Engagement

Announcement has been made of the engagement of Bonnie Joan Colwell and Joseph James DeAngelo, Jr. No definite date has been set for the wedding.

The bride elect is the daughter of Mr. and Mrs. Stanley B. Colwell of rural Auburn and the future bridegroom is the son of Mrs. Jack Bosanko of Auburn and Joseph J. DeAngelo, Sr. of Korea.

Miss Colwell was graduated from Del Oro High School and Sierra College where she is a lab assistant in the Science Department. She is affiliated with the Life Science Club, AGS (honor society) and the President's Honor Roll.

Young DeAngelo is a graduate of Folsom High School and Sierra College. He is employed by Sierra Crane and Hoist Co. of Newcastle. He is affiliated with the Vet's Club, AGS, President's Honor Roll and the International Diving Association, N.A.U.I.

## Job's Corner

Bethel No. 148, Auburn, held election of officers last

The CREEP Among Us * Anne Penn

The engagement announcement said:

Colwell DeAngelo Pair Announce Engagement –
The article states:

Announcement has been made of the engagement of Bonnie Jean Colwell and Joseph James DeAngelo Junior. No definite date has been set for the wedding.

The bride elect is the daughter of Mr. and Mrs. Stanley B. Colwell of rural Auburn and the future bridegroom is the son of Mrs. Jack Bosanko of Auburn and Joseph J. DeAngelo Sr. of Korea.

Miss Colwell was graduated from Del Oro High School and Sierra College where she is a lab assistant in the Science Department BLANK affiliated with the Life Science Club, AGS (honor society) and the President's Honor Roll.

Young DeAngelo is a graduate of Folsom High School and Sierra College. He is employed by Sierra Crane and Hoist Co. of Newcastle. He is affiliated with the Vet's Club, AGS, President's Honor Roll and the International Diving Association. N.A.U.I.

END OF ANNOUNCEMENT

The wedding never happened

One of the things that jumps out of course is the statement that DeAngelo actually graduated from Folsom High when in fact he got his GED before going into the Navy. The other thing is the fact that

JJD was involved in diving. In my previous book I mention he may have been involved in swimming.

ie Colwell marriage

It did not take Mr. DeAngelo long to date and then become engaged to his wife Sharon Huddle. She had also attended Sacramento State University. They wed November 10, 1973. JJD became a police officer moving to Exeter, CA just a few minutes' drive away from Visalia. His wife Sharon wanted to become a lawyer and attended law school.

Mrs. Joseph DeAngelo

### DeAngelo-Huddle

The Auburn First Congregational Church served as the setting for the marriage of Sharon Marie Huddle and Joseph James DeAngelo Jr.

She is the daughter of Mr. and Mrs. Clarence N. Huddle of Citrus Heights and his parents are Mrs. Jack Bosanko of Garden Grove and Joseph J. DeAngelo of Korea.

She is a graduate of San Juan High School and American River College. Her husband was graduated from Folsom High School and California State University, Sacramento.

Honor attendants were Patricia Huddle of Citrus Heights and Larry Schneider of Rancho Cordova.

Mrs. Joseph DeAngelo

Announcement DeAngelo-Huddle

The Auburn First Congregational Church served as the setting for the marriage of Sharon Marie Huddle and Joseph James DeAngelo Jr.

She is the daughter of Mr. and Mrs. Clarence N. Huddle of Citrus Heights and his parents are Mrs. Jack Bosanko of Garden Grove and Joseph J. DeAngelo of Korea.

She is a graduate of San Juan High School and American River College. Her husband graduated from Folsom High School and California State University, Sacramento.

Honor attendants were Patricia Huddle of Citrus Heights and Larry Schneider of Rancho Cordova.
END OF ANNOUNCEMENT

This church is right off Auburn Ravine Road in Auburn California. They were married prior to moving to Exeter, CA

According to reports from articles and research as far back as the DeAngelo's life in Auburn California here is what we can surmise. Not long after leaving Exeter and after purchasing a home in Auburn, CA the young couple already slept in separate bedrooms. DeAngelo's former Police Chief had come over to see the home DeAngelo had just purchased. DeAngelo gave him a tour saying this is my room and this is my wife's room. The DeAngelo's were married in November 1973. As soon as 1976 we know DeAngelo was committing rape attacks in Sacramento and two of those attacks were on his wedding anniversary with Sharon. 1976 and 1977. It is said the DeAngelo's separated in 1990 or 1991. The DeAngelo's lived in Auburn during the years 1976-1979 until JJD was fired for shoplifting. All of these things occurred and the crimes were committed prior to JJD becoming a father. I have intentionally left out much detail here as his daughters deserve some modicum of privacy.

Beginning in 1981 his first daughter was born. In 1986 his second daughter was born and in 1989 his third daughter came along. Not too much longer after that he and Sharon became separated. There was a restraining order filed at some point for domestic issues.

Prior to the separation of JJD and his wife and according to the neighbors the couple had very loud and angry shouting matches. JJD's wife lived separately from him but when he came to her home some the neighbors stated he would yell and scream from the driveway and never step inside. Their relationship was described as volatile and very toxic. JJD would swear frequently. A neighbor knew the household was not stable so he did not let his children interact with their children. Neighbors also describe JJD's wife as a person who always kept to herself.

Within days of JJD's arrest his estranged wife officially closed down her law office. Records indicate it was closed as of May 4, 2018.

## The CREEP Among Us * Anne Penn

Joseph DeAngelo secured a position at a Roseville, CA distribution center for Save Mart grocery store working there for 27 years. According to coworkers JJD did nothing to make anyone suspect that he could ever have any connection to the crimes he is accused of. JJD had begun his time there in 1990. Co-workers saw a family man in JJD.

Some of JJD's neighbors saw another side to this man saying he even went so far as to threaten the neighbors' dog. JJD said "If you don't shut that dog up I'm going to bring a load of death to your house."

Charlies café owner Charlene Carte said that DeAngelo who was a frequent diner there. She nicknamed JJD Mr. Happy because of his grumpy demeanor. It was stated that JJD was known as a difficult customer with odd food requests.

A birthday party a DeAngelo daughter attended as a child was notable because of JJD's behavior which was very, very abrasive and scary to the children. The neighbor did not have them over again.

In spite of his disposition people in Citrus Heights were shocked to hear of DeAngelo's arrest and the charges filed against him.

There is so much more detail that is known via many, many sources at this point as people have written articles and posted things here and there on social media that have to do with DeAngelo and his family. I will not invade their privacy any more than the brief descriptions of parents, and his spouse that I have mentioned here.

# The CREEP Among Us * Anne Penn

The CREEP Among Us * Anne Penn

## Crimes in Citrus Heights After 1980

"I found this article about a series of home invasion rapes in Citrus Heights between August and November 1981. JJD's first daughter was born in Sacramento 9/9/81. The attacker wore a ski mask during the attacks and tried to drag one of the victim's outside.hmm.. That is the Greenleaf neighborhood of attack #9." (Proboarder)

### Three Assaulted In Citrus Heights

*[newspaper clipping]*

This article was found by a proboarder

Authorities are seeking a man who has reportedly broken into three Citrus Heights homes and sexually assaulted three young girls in an area north of Madison Avenue and between Dewey Drive and San Juan Avenue, Sherriff's Lt. Ray Biondi said Monday.

Root said the suspect entered all three homes between 2 a.m. and 4 a.m. between late August and early November. He raped the first woman, an 18-

year-old. In the second attack he tried to drag a 17 year-old out of the home and fled when she resisted. In the last attack he was interrupted when a 14-year-old girl's sister returned home. Authorities are not certain if the same man is responsible for the last attack. Because the girl described him as being older than the first suspect described by the first two victims. But because it happened only a few blocks from the other attacks Root said detectives believe it may be the same man. The man wore a ski mask during the attacks and is believed to be between 18 and 26 years old. END OF ARTICLE

# The CREEP Among Us * Anne Penn

## Sue's Story 1983

I moved to the Sacramento area in 1981 as my husband was stationed at McClellan AFB as medical personnel and a captain. We lived in the Rollingwood Apts. on Madison just west of Main in Orangevale for 2 years...Then we bought a house in Orangevale on Butterwood Circle in the Rollingwood subdivision right next to the apts complex...and our circle was the last one off of Blue Oak (which comes off of Madison Ave) near Main.. Moved into this corner home in 83 with a VA loan....It had been on the market for a while due to a recession

....On Thanksgiving Eve a few months after moving in, my husband awoke to see a masked man standing at the end of our bed watching us. He pretended to be asleep and was trying to see if he had a weapon. It was dark as our porch light was out and it was raining. I was asleep. The man rummaged on the dresser, & then with a gloved hand pulled back the curtains to the sliding glass door a bit and gazed into our backyard and then back to end of bed, almost like he was thinking according to my husband. He then faded out. My husband clutched my arm and urgently whispered, get up, get up, there's a man in the house...call the police. He rolled off the bed (on hands and knees to see if man was in bedroom before slamming the bedroom doors) as I called the police. As I was talking to the Sheriff dispatcher my husband slammed the double doors to our master bedroom and locked it and then the dispatcher said to me

## The CREEP Among Us * Anne Penn

"Ma'am please be quiet. Someone is listening on your extension." The other phone was in our kitchen. Then she said, the deputies are almost there. We know now she may have saved our lives as they didn't get there for 20 minutes...but the man left and the paper boy reported to our neighbors next door the next morning a masked man was on the fence between our homes at 5 am. The deputies said, "he'll be back." We had never heard of the East Area Rapist and the deputies never mentioned that either. We spent Thanksgiving putting extra locks on the doors, borrowed a gun from a military friend and we slept from then on locked in our bedroom and took turns in shifts sitting up with the gun every night. The next week we had an alarm that calls police installed and went on to get our own guns that we slept with.

The following week at 3:30 am... there was a loud pounding on our door...my husband took the gun and ran and looked out the peep hole staring right at the man at the door. He described him as hair parted in middle, dark blonde, to his collar, 5'10 and about 170 which he said was much like his own size. There was an older model sedan light colored with what appeared to be a man driving idling in front of our house. He threw open the door and pointed the gun at the man. I was cowering in the hallway shouting don't open the door, but he did and I heard him yelling words. The man ran to get into the car and stood there staring him down before jumping in and it did a U turn and took off........then the door slammed and I looked out and my husband was in our car chasing the other car...He chased them down Main Avenue, to Hazel, and back to Highway 50 before losing them to high speed...

Fast forward to 4 weeks ago when I watched the Golden State Killer on TV...I then googled the term and found out all about the East Area Rapist and looked up where his attacks were.... I was astounded two attacks (and the first one on a couple) were right across the street from our house which was on Butterwood Circle in Orangevale. (Blue Oak that Butterwood Circle comes off of right next to Main crosses Main and becomes Buffalo Way. Shortly make right on Dredgewood and immediate left is Richdale and he attacked the corner house there in 1977....

I contacted by email my ex-husband and told him to watch the special...that I thought this so called East Area Rapist that had been in the Sacramento area in the late 70s was the man in our house...he did and agreed! ...he then looked at the composites on the FBI website and without hesitation picked out the middle one and since the arrest has said that was the man now arrested was the one at our door that night banging on it.... I was at a lunch meeting the day before the arrest in which the DA was the speaker. I was able to tell her our story and that we wanted her to know we think that was him in our house in 83 (during the quiet time) and that he was here in Sacramento still or returned to visit family for Thanksgiving...& that my husband had seen his face! I sent what happened to her lead investigator.... she didn't bat an eye..because she knew it was possible that he was still in the area because he was and was ...living 15 minutes from our home which was near two previous attacks.........and that he was going to be arrested the next day.! ..It was shocking to me that next day I hear an arrest!

Then I find out where he lived all those years & he went to the same grocery store I did for years...Bel Air store at Sunrise and Cirby..and in fall of 83 I was building a veterinary hospital in the shopping center and we were there every evening after work to check out the progress of the building....I also had a vet hospital near Main avenue at Greenback & Madison I opened in 82 the year before which is in a center anchored with an Albertson's grocery store...(Save Mart where the EAR worked 27 years bought out Albertson's)

.....Through another group, the now 40 year old daughter of one of my staff at the vet hospital on Madison and Greenback told me they had a masked man in their home which is off on Oak Avenue Parkway near Main (about 10 minutes from the EAR house he was arrested in) in early 84..They were also new to the area and just now learned of the EAR and thought back like we did since the arrest........In their case her father woke up and saw him trying to get one of his guns...they had two big dogs that started growling and barking and he ran out and into the girls bedroom...She saw him crouching at end of her bed, dropped the gun on her bed and went out her window....

We all now wonder if he didn't follow us from a grocery store or from one of the vet hospitals. My partner in the Sunrise Cirby vet hospital lived 2 streets north of the EAR for 10 years....and we had several friends who lived in the subdivision. We moved from the that house in 1987. After putting all of this together after all of these years.... I have read Murder On His Mind Serial Killer, Case Files,

McNamara book, Sudden Terror and Hunting a Psychopath and googled everything I can find on the subject.......I still sleep with a loaded gun under my pillow, keep all the lights on inside and outside my house, double pad locked side gates that are high and with flood lights and cameras... and have dogs and an alarm that calls cops....and am glad he was captured.

My heart goes out to the attacked and terrorized victims and to those who lost their lives to this monster as well as the poor families that have suffered so much....I hope they find some solace in seeing him in that cage and he will never get out.... Just what happened to us scared us so much it took years to not think of it and to sleep normally. & we didn't even know who this was at the time...just a burglar... Rekindling memories has brought it all back and reading the files.... We now know we were so lucky nothing worse happened and that we are alive.

## Chapter Thirteen

### The DNA joining with Genealogy sites

The beginnings of getting closer to finding the CREEP.

Back in 2001 this article made us aware that DNA linked EAR to ONS:

My comment: We had to wait another seventeen long years more to find the answers after this announcement.

2001 article DNA Links '70s 'East Area Rapist' to Serial Killings / Evidence suggests suspect moved to Southern California

**Erin Hallissy and Charlie Goodyear, Chronicle Staff Writers**
**Published 4:00 am PDT, Wednesday, April 4, 2001**

"The East Area Rapist forged a trail of terror from Sacramento to San Ramon in the late 1970s, randomly breaking into women's homes and raping them while their husbands were kept silent.
Just as suddenly as he began his spree of 40 rapes, the attacker disappeared at the end of the decade without ever being identified.

Now, through recently analyzed DNA evidence, the Contra Costa County crime lab has linked the notorious East Area Rapist with an elusive serial killer who slew 10 people in Southern California coastal communities between 1979 and 1986.

The rapist-killer's identity is still unknown, but police say it is clear that the same man, described in police records as methodical, sexually deviant and with above-average intelligence, committed all the crimes. It is a finding that has relieved investigators, who thought they would never solve the cases, and also has worried them, because the man remains unidentified."

RAPIST MOVES TO CONTRA COSTA
"By 1978, the rapist started hitting Contra Costa County, attacking women in Concord, Danville and San Ramon.
"He would go into nice homes, usually occupied by a man and a woman," said **Karen Sheldon**, director of the Contra Costa Sheriff's Department crime lab. "He would tie up the male. He then put dishes or something on his back so there would be noise if the guy moved while the suspect was committing the rape. I think he liked to have a man present. He enjoyed the risk."

The rapist frequently threatened to kill both the man and woman if the dishes fell off and broke.
A task force was formed to try to solve the crimes, said District Attorney Gary Yancey, but leads fizzled out, and, although some suspects were investigated, no one was charged."
*For the full article go to: https://www.sfgate.com/news/article/DNA-Links-70s-East-Area-Rapist-to-Serial-2935342.php

Fast forward the 17 additional years while controversy surrounded the case and finally people had spoken about this creep. They talked about how he still needed to be found and brought to justice. It was obvious for the last several years that a Familial DNA match would most likely find the creep we searched for. The ability has been there for quite some time. GEDmatch came on scene via the internet in about 2010.

GEDmatch is "an open data personal genomics database and genealogy website. "Its main purpose is to help amateur and professional researchers and genealogists." GEDmatch users can upload their autosomal DNA profile from commercial DNA companies, with or without a GEDCOM file, to identify potential relatives who had also uploaded their profile".

So essentially what happened in the Joseph DeAngelo DNA search was that Law Enforcement uploaded his DNA profile to GEDmatch. It identified 10 to 20 distant relatives of the Golden State Killer/Original Night Stalker/East Area Rapist. A team of five investigators used this information to construct a family tree. The search went back several generations to DeAngelo's great, great, great grandfather. Law Enforcement would need and would use an expert genealogist to help trace DeAngelo's family tree to present times. The expert who worked this case recently allowed herself to be identified as the woman behind the scenes who helped capture DeAngelo. Her name is Barbara Rae-Venter. Working from her home she had been helping adoptees use DNA to find their birth parents.

The story goes that Paul Holes contacted Rae-Venter in March 2017 and she began to work the case in October of that same year. She personally researched the cases and found what we knew, that this was an evil monster she was trying to track down.

As it turned out Ventura County had an untouched sample from Charlene Smith's rape from March 1980 that had been stored in the Ventura County crime lab. In January 2018 the data came in showing the long lineage they would have to trace to present times in order to find the killer. Using family tree building software about two dozen trees had to be built. It took several months but at one point based on knowledge from old crime scenes, descriptions and areas the suspect may have lived Rae-Venter determined the guy had a fair amount of Italian in him".

Finally, the list was narrowed down to nine names, a second cousin offered to be tested and she came back as his second cousin on his mother's side of the family. In April the suspect list was down to six men and DeAngelo was one. All of these years I have believed the man had blue eyes based on witness descriptions as the monster had glared at the victims through the eye holes of a ski mask. When looked at, the remaining six men, only one had blue eyes and that was DeAngelo. He became the number one suspect. The investigators had looked at DeAngelo's driver's license from DMV records, he was the guy they would now surveil. Watching him for one-day shy of a week DeAngelo did not spot them, did not appear to notice Law Enforcement as they followed him around Citrus Heights. Using a discarded tissue, they tested and compared the DNA to his profile which came back as a 100% DNA match. The warrant was issued for his arrest which came on April 24, 2018. They came to arrest the perpetrator at long last. You are under arrest and after the statements made to him while arresting him were done DeAngelo's reply was "I have a roast in the oven." DeAngelo was booked into the Sacramento County jail at 2:29 a.m. April 25, 2018.

The CREEP Among Us * Anne Penn

This is an example only and is not representative of the DeAngelo case. It comes from another case in Washington State graphics by Mark Nowlin The Seattle Times reporting by Sara Jean Green and the source is the Snohomish Sheriff's Office:

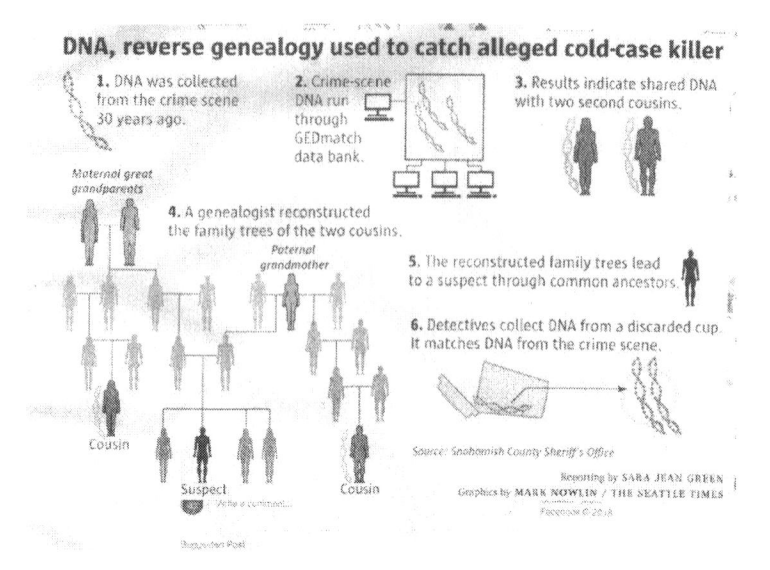

**DNA, reverse genealogy used to catch alleged cold-case killer**

1. DNA was collected from the crime scene 30 years ago.
2. Crime-scene DNA run through GEDmatch data bank.
3. Results indicate shared DNA with two second cousins.
4. A genealogist reconstructed the family trees of the two cousins.
5. The reconstructed family trees lead to a suspect through common ancestors.
6. Detectives collect DNA from a discarded cup. It matches DNA from the crime scene.

Source: Snohomish County Sheriff's Office
Reporting by SARA JEAN GREEN
Graphics by MARK NOWLIN / THE SEATTLE TIMES

This chart/graphic was posted publicly on Facebook. This simple visual explains the way DNA was used to find the perpetrator. In Joseph James DeAngelo's case the sample used for comparison to the JJD DNA profile came from a semen sample converted to download on GED Match. The sample taken from the rape of Charlene Smith in 1980. A good sample was left in Ventura County's possession 38 years after the murders of my uncle Lyman Robert Smith and his wife Charlene March 13, 1980.

Once they figured out via the reverse genealogy who their likely suspect was JJD was placed under surveillance. While under surveillance a tissue was tossed by JJD which was then used to compare the DNA from the tissue to the profile that has been in the possession of Law Enforcement since the 1970's via rape kits.

The cooperative effort between Law Enforcement and a Genealogical expert was very welcome after 42 years. In an article about the process to find the criminal, and our search for so long to find a missing piece to the puzzle in walks the marriage of DNA profiles and people who are experts at building family trees. This has been available for several years on sites like Ancestry and others. Our ability as humans to trace our ancestors and our roots back hundreds of years has always been something that I was interested in and fascinated by.

Over time criminal DNA databases produced no hits at all. One of the reasons I was convinced he had never been in any real trouble. No felonies and certainly none that had him in prison. The criminal always wore gloves, never left any prints anywhere. I mention in my previous books that he may have noticed that reports of Ted Bundy's crimes talked about how there were never any fingerprints left at his crime scenes. Ted Bundy was so meticulous about leaving no trace, not only did he wear gloves he also wiped down every place he stayed and every crime scene. Trouble was there were bits of evidence left in the cars Ted used to abduct and transport his victims. But then DeAngelo was a cop. He did not need Ted Bundy to figure out how to elude capture after all.

Paul Holes from Contra Costa County Crime Lab, a man who was a DNA expert talked for quite some time about downloading the culprits' DNA profile into a DNA profiling site. I think the idea came to him in about 2013. That is speculation on my part. The point is that it was something talked about for several years before it was actually done. That site ended up being GED Match. GED Match has different privacy laws than some of the companies out there. The downloaded profile matched relatives from the suspects family going back to his great, great, great grandparents who lived in the 1800's. Twenty-Five trees had to be created which involved thousands of relatives connected to the killer present day. The initial DNA identified distant relatives but not a suspect. Tracing this family trees in this way requires artistry and determination. Using obituaries, census records and other databases to trace the connections, after about four months of dogged pursuit through the generations they found DeAngelo who now sits in jail.

The genealogy trail lead LE at last to their suspect. The trees led first to nine men who were on the suspect list, then it was whittled down to six. Based on DMV records only one, Joseph James DeAngelo had blue eyes. After surveilling him and gathering a tissue discarded by DeAngelo, the test of his DNA came back as a 100% match as discussed earlier in this book. The expert genealogist who worked this case had been horrified at the evil behavior of the predator she helped law enforcement find at last.

## Chapter Fourteen

## Who is Anne Penn aka Laurie?

For those of you who have not read my previous books about this case I must tell you who I am and why I have been greatly interested in the resolve of these cases. Knowing who I am will also help explain why I care so much about how this criminal was not stopped in the beginning of his crimes. So many people have, and had a serious interest in catching this guy. The trail of terro and debris left in the wake of JJD was enormous. Hundreds of people needed resolve in this case. If JJD had been found in the first six years of his crimes at least ten people could still be with us.

We cannot go back and change what has happened even though that would certainly be great. I do not fault the original investigators of these crimes. They did the best they could at the time with the resources they had. I have discussed this in the volume here. I am and have been very grateful to all people who choose law enforcement as a career. It has to be one of the most difficult of professions over time. The cost to them personally and as individuals as well as the cost to their families over time is enormous. I just wish as anyone who has been involved with these cases that we had stopped him early on before he did so much damage to so many people and their loved ones.

The following is what I had written in my previous book which was written prior to JJD's arrest.

I am attached to this case for two reasons. I was there in Sacramento, a young 19-year-old single woman living alone when JJD began his attacks as EAR. And then after he left Sacramento less than two years later this is what happened:

"The fact is that my grandfather's son Lyman Robert Smith was a murder victim along with his wife Charlene Smith in Ventura County, California. They were murdered on March 13, 1980.

This case, these serial rapes and then murders were personal. They are still personal not only to me and to the Lyman Smith family, but they certainly are to all of the other victims in these cases all over the state of California. These cases are personal to the communities, and in the communities in which they happened. If you lived in Sacramento through the attacks in 1976-1978 you will understand the terror that came into our town and you will understand the fear associated with this case that was felt by everyone. Especially felt by the young women and girls that were there for the two years of unrelenting attacks. Especially felt by all of the victims in every county as EAR moved about in their towns and in their homes.

Consider being terrorized and then within about a year and a half after EAR seemingly stopped his attacks in your town you discover your grandfather's son and his wife are murdered. They were murdered by an unknown assailant who beat them to death with a log in their own bedroom. A murderer who may have watched as they were intimate for what would be the last time. Consider watching up close the absolute fallout that happens when someone you love loses someone they love. This was the case for me. I had to watch my grandfather try to live with not only the loss of his son and Charlene, but the way in which they were lost that one could not comprehend. A murderer was still free after all these years and he had an effect on many people. I finally was compelled to write about the case and who I thought the man was all those years ago because I wanted to tell my thoughts about where the criminal came from and where I still thought the East Area Rapist/Original Night Stalker was. I wanted to get the word out to the good people of Sacramento because my gut told me he was still there. His arrogance was the main reason I thought he had stayed.

I was born at Mather Air Force Base and lived in Sacramento all of my life. My family bought the house in South Sacramento in 1956. My grandmother had quite a lot of input about where my parents purchased their home so that it and we would be close to her.

In February 1956 while my mother was barely pregnant with me my grandmother Veonia lost her husband of 17 years. He passed away from a heart issue, dying in my uncle's arms in their living room. By the time I was born that same year my parents had already purchased the house in South Sacramento which was off the 47$^{th}$ Avenue exit off highway 99. My grandmother lived just off the 12$^{th}$ Avenue Exit on West Curtis Park. She was alone there in the house her husband had purchased in 1928. The home had a very nice view of Curtis Park. It was close to Hughes Stadium and to Land Park. The Highway 99 freeway is one block away.

While my mother and father were busy adding children having my younger brother by March 1958 my grandmother was trying to get over the loss of my biological grandfather. She traveled; she socialized realizing that if she kept moving that she would somehow be able to get through her loss.

In 1956 Lyman Jones Smith lost his wife Wilma to cancer. He had one grown son and another teen aged son. Their names are Lyman Robert and Donald Roger. I am certain he was very devastated by the loss of his wife and it took him a while to process his grief.

I am not certain of exactly where Lyman Jones Smith and Veonia met, but both loved to have fun, loved to laugh, and by June 1960 they married one another having fallen in love. They were very happy. This is one of the first family events I actually remember because weddings are a big deal. My grandparents wedding took place at the First Baptist Church in downtown Sacramento and the reception was at the Lanai off Freeport Blvd. in Sacramento June 26, 1960. I was three.

I am connected to this story like it or not. The story is certainly not one that a person would choose. It was never on my list to talk about much less write about. As a matter of fact, I never told anyone about the murders except my husband who wanted to know why I was so uncomfortable with shades not drawn at dark or sliding glass doors that did not at least have security locks or sticks in them.

Finally, I felt compelled to write what I think. As it turns out doing this has had a healing element in the process as I have looked back at my past and the really wonderful relationship I had with Lyman Jones and Veonia Smith. These two people were more like my own parents than grandparents. I do not know how I could have gotten through my childhood without them.

As I have said, what motivated me originally to write about this subject was the fact that I wanted to pay tribute to Lyman Robert and Charlene as well as all of the victims including the ones who survived. At least the survivors were able to go on to write their own stories, have their own lives. The murder victims abruptly had their stories and what they were to become stolen from them by this serial murderer.

I have always had an innate curiosity about everything since I was born. I have always wanted to know why things are the way they are and why something happens. I have always asked why, but this particular subject and this particular story I had avoided like the plague. Too frightening, too dark it was a part of the past that I had tried to forget.

But then there is the part of me that never forgot, that looked at and studied serial killers. Since 1980 I have been researching serial killers, and studied the mindset of serial killers and others who commit murder more than once. Everyone who has ever known me has joked about this dark obsession. By the end of 1980 I began reading and researching information that we as a society knew about serial killers in particular. The murders of Lyman and Charlene appeared to be random from my perspective and it did not make sense to me that the murders would have been committed by someone they knew. Although Law Enforcement always looks at who the victims knew and those closest to them it just did not make sense to me. Especially when the Joseph Alsip case was dropped and the case essentially went cold as soon as they in Law Enforcement thought Alsip was the perpetrator in 1980. Alsip was released in 1982 after having been arrested in 1981. It is important to know and remember that the charges against Mr. Alsip were dropped and dismissed. The case never went to trial. They lacked any evidence. They spent an entire year of court time trying to determine if Mr. Alsip's Pastor was a reliable witness against him.

As a child I watched as everyone else did the story of the Manson murders unfold. This was my second experience learning about the bizarre behaviors of others who seemingly kill at random and in the most horrific of ways. The first experience was in 1963 when the murder of our President from a sniper's bullets' shook everyone. In 1968 Bobby Kennedy was murdered and so was Dr. Martin Luther King. We were in the middle of Vietnam, race riots and unrest in general. There were the Zodiac murders and that unknown assailant is still free. The craziness of the times became the norm.

The Smith murders to me seemed more like a crazed individual. The sheer brutality of how Lyman and Charlene were killed seemed more in line with a random act or a serial killer. I wrote about my impressions of the man, the murderer, criminal, rapist, terrorist who was still free until April 24, 2018. The victims of these crimes were I think randomly picked by this criminal and were unfortunate enough to be picked at their most vulnerable. I am certain it was no accident that this criminal stalked all of his victims, chose them, watched them and set up the crimes so that he had the best chance not only of surprising them, but of obtaining and keeping control.

It was no accident that he waited until the couples in most cases had settled down for the night. I can picture him waiting and watching until these couples were asleep just long enough to have settled into a deep enough sleep to be the absolute most vulnerable that they could be. He wanted to make sure they were confused and hazy. When a man such as this comes into our awareness terrorizing and killing the people we love the stories do appeal to the fear in most of us. We should be afraid of the inhuman perpetrators of violent crimes.

There are many, many victims of violent crimes out there who have to figure out how to live every day, how to move on and how to live with such horrible memories and horrible visualizations of things that no one should have to experience or recall. Some people were lucky in the beginning to walk away from this madman. As this criminal fine tuned his game some were not so lucky."

** I also must say that JJD is somewhat different than other serial killers in that he could change his MO, and in addition to being a self preservation killer, in my opinion also would attack or attack and kill people who may have crossed him in some way. A revenge type type of attacker. This is one of the reasons I still search for a connection to my Uncle Lyman, My grandfather Lyman Senior, and ask myself and others if they might have run across one another somewhere in Sacramento and if there truly is some connection rather than a random one. It is conceivable to me that JJD was enraged or angry at Lyman Senior possibly. They worked in the same area of Roseville/Citrus Heights.

Another connection is this: In the late 1970's, meaning around 1974 – 1979, within this time frame my grandparents had contracting work done on their master bedroom. A worker/contractor came into their home and converted a closet into a bathroom. If JJD was doing contract work and had been in my grandparents home he would have had the opportunity to see Lyman and Charlene's photograph. He would also have likely spoken to my grandparents as the job was being done. My grandmother had what they call the gift of gab. Did she tell this worker about what Lyman Robert for a living and mentioned where they lived? Did she mention Lyman lived in Sanata Paula? She would not have thought anything of it as she was friendly abd was proud of her step son and Charlene. It would not have been too hard to track them down. We may never know, but I do still wonder.

**And Now after arrest of JJD**: As we know now the East Area Rapist had already murdered in Visalia in 1975 prior to arriving in Sacramento. DeAngelo has been charged for the Maggiore murders in Sacramento from February 1978 as well as Professor Claude Snelling from Visalia in 1975. That was not enough as the first three murders appear to have been self-preservation murders. He really wanted the ultimate scene he had prepared in his mind to finally kill several couples up close and personal by blunt force trauma. Rape was also part of the fantasy in some of the murders that he kept control of, but it was not what drove him. At the end of his spree he went back to killing two more women who happened to be alone on the nights he struck. He began in Goleta which is in Santa Barbara County. He continued to destroy lives in Ventura, California and then in Laguna Niguel in Orange County, California. This was not enough. He went back to Goleta to murder three more people over the course of the next year and a half. He murdered from the end of 1979 until towards the end of 1981. Then, apparently the killing stopped.

Five years would go by before the next murder that we know of and the victim was back in Irvine California less than two miles from the murder scene of Manuela Witthuhn. Janelle Cruz would be the serial killer's youngest victim in May 1986. He would have the last word. As far as we know the killer has stopped for the last thirty years. END OF PREVIOUS DESCRIPTION FROM MY PRIOR BOOKS

And now... we will have the last word. "What is justice when you've lost a family member to murder?" Our grandfather, Lyman Smith Senior would be relieved and glad that his son and Charlene will receive justice so totally deserved although so delayed.

## The CREEP Among Us * Anne Penn

Lyman Jones Smith Senior in the kitchen Curtis Park 1992 (I took the picture). You can still see the twinkle in his eye. Lyman lived until 2001 to the great age of 92 almost 93. It is conceivable that his son Lyman Robert could have still been alive today had he and Charlene not been taken by the CREEP.

Footnote: There are so many people who were affected by these crimes over a lifetime. Each person has a story. Many were told and some will never be. Each story deserves to be told and to be listened to. My books were written to try to rid myself of the demon, the dark story that I lived with from the time I was 19 until what I am now, an almost 62-year-old woman. Think about how very long we all worried and wondered. This man never physically touched me, he just touched my mind and kept me wary of strangers and any preconceived threat. Hypervigilant, I tried to be safe so I could live my life. There are hundreds of women in these cases who know exactly what I am talking about and some who know more than the rest of us. I shudder to think of the many victims who experienced this evil first hand. My heart goes out to them, my prayers have been with them all from the beginning. It is my hope that healing will continue for everyone connected to this most terrible story. Best Regards and Best Wishes. Like the words of Bruce Harrington at the press conference after the arrest of DeAngelo, Mr. Harrington applauded law enforcement's pursuit of justice for them. DeAngelo's arrest, he said, will "bring closure to the anguish that we all suffered for the last 40-odd years. Sleep Better Tonight, He Isn't Coming Through The Window'

Thank you to all who have read these books, thank you to all who have reached out and helped me travel this road, especially in the last three years.

As a side note:

How I found out about the arrest

In a way I wanted to simultaneously know everything and nothing about the creep. I was angry. That was a surprisingly first reaction to the news. The very first seconds I was skeptical. Is this for real? It sounds vague and I was not sure. Long ago I had learned to temper my reactions so I would not be disappointed. When victims and families wait this long, this 42 years, 38 years, 32 years, and it went on and on one becomes guarded and skeptical at any news, any progress.

I have to say that I could not figure out in the last two to three years why it was taking so long to track this man's DNA. They talked about it for quite some time. Everyone said "well we have his DNA" My thought was always "Well what are you waiting for?" I realized that there are privacy issues about ancestry sites and whether or not one could be allowed to go hunting in this somewhat virtual world even if one is looking for a serial killer.

From what I had read it was open to those with a search warrant. The ancestry sites and genealogical sites did mostly say that if they were approached with a search warrant they certainly would cooperate. If law enforcement was looking for a non-descript person with no name that anyone actually knew it became tricky. How does one go fishing for a man with no name that is attached to the DNA profile in their possession?

This is how we will do things moving forward. There will be litigation most likely quickly in order to make sure agencies follow what laws they conceive of in order to make sure their search is lawful. No one wants cases to be thrown out because a judge decides the way the evidence (DNA) and the match have come about are not lawful.

The universe had me in Sacramento when the news came to me. I was in Sacramento for the first time to visit old friends having not been there for this purpose for decades. Each time I had been back to Sacramento I had come on a mission to take pictures or have a quick lunch with someone. Once my grandparents had passed away my trips to the valley for holidays were more limited. Mostly I had driven through over the years or stopped to see or do one thing, exiting quickly.

On April 24, 2018 I had lunch with my father in the area, stopped to see old friends out near Del Paseo Heights and before dark drove out Highway 99 towards Elk Grove to see my old friend Kathleen. I was to spend the night with her. It was getting late so I asked her if I could use her computer briefly as I had not even wanted to bring a laptop or device with me. I had been out of touch all day. At half past midnight I looked at Facebook, and then looked at the proboards briefly. It was instant. I saw and knew something was going on. A news report had mentioned there may be or possibly was a man being arrested. I sat there looking, reading. I called out, Kathleen they may have caught him, this might be solved. She and I both thought and said, "this is surreal" The fact that I was with her now at this moment was like coming full circle. The beginning of my fear had happened in 1971 when I was chased down on my own street by two men in a truck, I ran, but could not make it home. Instead I had run to Kathleen's house, putting my body between the screen door and door as I yelled help please open the door.

It was Kathleen and her mother Esther who opened the door, who saved me from the terror I was running from. This was when fear came to live inside my mind, in my bones. Now here I was in Kathleen's home in Elk Grove, one I had not seen in almost 25 years when the news came that the man who had ravaged my fear and fight or flight responses over time was being arrested as we watched in real time. This man with the initials JJD was booked at 2:30 a.m. We watched as the booking sheet was posted for all to see in real time.

I was sent a message by Morf. Don't worry Anne, this is for real 100% DNA match. It was 3:00 a.m. I could go to sleep. I did not have to worry about the locks on all the doors and windows so much and I could sleep. Tomorrow would bring the announcements from all of the different jurisdictions that the man they had in custody was the serial killer known as first The East Area Rapist, and then the Original Night Stalker. Now as I finally gave up my fight at rebranding a serial killer as though it would somehow help to catch him, The Golden State Killer was behind bars. Arrested by the very county he had first terrorized in 1976. His captors could flip the light on if they wanted to while he was the one asleep. The cops he had manipulated and taunted now had the power to blind him with the light whenever they pleased. He at last has no control, no power over the last remaining years of his life.

JJD thinks he has something left to bargain with. It is my initial feeling that the criminal will wait. He will see where this takes him and use whatever bargaining chips he thinks he has in order to trade them for safety. He will want to trade information eventually for the right place to reside and to live out his final days in captivity. He knows that if he goes out into the general population in any prison system he would be a target. Ex-cop, rapist, hurter of young girls 12 years old and up, serial killer and evil doer. He knows he would not last long in the prison system among "regular" criminals and creeps. Like Dahmer, he would get his

## Thank You's and Acknowledgments

I must thank my patient family as this case continued to take up time and space. The reasons it continued were great ones as the arrest had finally come. The reactions I had after the arrest, emotions that came up and surprised me as I tried to and still try to process this story and the very new outcome. When one knows a story this well and for so many years it takes time to get the fact that the ending to the story has changed and will continue to change. We now know who the suspect is. The story did not end with us never knowing who the man of our creepy nightmares was and is.

So, I must thank people I have an infinite amount of gratitude and respect for. Besides my family, first I must thank Larry Crompton who has always done anything he can to help victims and victims family members even after he has been retired from Contra Costa County Law Enforcement. He has never ceased to fight for the victims and to fight to get the word out to solve these crimes while we are all still here. Thank you to his family as well for sharing him and his expertise, his diplomacy and his persistence to get the job done. Larry dedicated so much of his time to this cause. More than that Larry Crompton is a very empathetic human who cared deeply about the outcome of this terrible series of murders and attacks. I can never repay him for his concern, his patience and his willingness to help. The world truly would be a much better place if we were fortunate enough to have more men like him on the planet. Thank you Larry Crompton (and Barb).

I must thank Mark Smith for some of the very same reasons I mentioned in the former paragraph. Mark has always listened, offered words of encouragement and helped in any way he could without question. So many times when I would ask, and discuss things on my mind, asking him to read this or look at that his reply was always, OK. Giving his time, his consideration, his logic and his human touch to this case as at times he endlessly listened to me or discussed with me, I also cannot thank him enough for his time and patience. I asked him a few times, "how did you get involved in this case?" "Why does this case matter to you?" He said he had heard about it and wanted the creep caught.

Some men want justice especially for female victims of violent crime. Mark is one of those men. Mark helped me research addresses, cross referenced directories from the 1970's and offered ballistics advice patiently trying to teach me what in the heck he was talking about. Mark also offered levity and a great sense of humor when one was desperately needed. This case is very dark and very serious. Mark knew when to throw in a disarming comment or would tell me to watch a very weird or funny YouTube clip. Thank you Mark Smith.

Thank you as well to so many sleuths that have become my friends. All offered support and encouragement when things could and did get tough. Golden State Killer Sleuths, East Area Rapist Golden

State Killer After The Arrest, and Golden State Killerinos. Eileen Mihalko, Dr.Sue Barrett, Kevin Sullivan, Pamela Simone, Kathleen Vincent. Grace Bissenden, Jodie Lebid, Lisa Smith, Jodie Mead, Julie Scroggins, Tracy Hart, Leigh Belken, marie Touhey Palhie, and Dan Zupansky as well as Mia, Cleopatra, Port, and early on Mel. Thank you all for all of your help during this journey. I cannot express my gratitude enough.

I also want to thank the Sacramento County District Attorney's office, Anne Marie Schubert, Thienvu Ho, Deputy District Attorney, Amy M. Holliday, Supervising Deputy District Attorney who will prosecute the case in Sacramento. Also thank you Joanie. The kindness shown to me by this great team was truly appreciated more than I can express.

I also want to thank all of the Law Enforcement investigators from all of the jurisdictions who never gave up on these cases even after some had retired. Passing the baton to the next team who came in. Thank you to the FBI who came back into the case in 2016 saying they thought this was solvable.

Thank you to Larry Pool, Senior Investigator - Riverside County District Attorney's Office - OCRCFL Orange County, Erica Hutchcraft, Orange County, California District Attorney Investigator, Paul Holes Contra Costa County Retired Criminalist and Investigator for the DA's Office, Paul Belli, Sacramento County Sheriff's, Mark Knutsen, FBI Field office Roseville, CA and Carol Daly retired Detective Sacramento County Sheriffs. There are countless law enforcement detectives, officers and others who never quit in their pursuit of EAR, ONS, VR and GSK I cannot list them all here. Thank you to all.

Thank you to Retired Police Chief Nick Willick for speaking with me and helping to shed light on how JJD was missed in Auburn, CA. I appreciate that more than you will know. Thank you also to Farrel Ward also a retired Officer from Exeter, CA who also was kind enough to speak with me to help me understand how things were in the 70's and why JJD was missed in Exeter.

Thank you as well to all of my old friends in Sacramento who like me were there in the 1970's, 1960's when this creep arrived. Thank you for reading my books and trying to help me in some way to get the word out about the criminal still being in Sacramento. Thank you to one of the Sacramento 70's Facebook sites as well.

We shall see how this story progresses and then how it will ultimately pass into history.

## The CREEP Among Us * Anne Penn

There are so very many victims of violent crimes in the United States. In particular, there are so many crimes against women in this country and around the globe. There are missing and exploited children, victims of sexual assault, murders, rapes and the list goes on.

## SEXUAL VIOLENCE

According to the National Crime Victimization Survey, which includes crimes that were *not* reported to the police, 232,960 women in the U.S. were raped or sexually assaulted in 2006. That's more than 600 women every day.[1] Other estimates, such as those generated by the FBI, are much lower because they rely on data from law enforcement agencies. A significant number of crimes are never even reported for reasons that include the victim's feeling that nothing can/will be done and the personal nature of the incident.[2]

## MURDER

In 2005, 1,181 women were murdered by an intimate partner.[1] That's an average of three women every day. Of all the women murdered in the U.S., about one-third were killed by an intimate partner. That of course means that the other two thirds were murdered by someone other than an intimate partner.

## THE TARGETS

Young women, low-income women and some minorities are disproportionately victims of domestic violence and rape. Women ages 20-24 are at greatest risk of nonfatal domestic violence, and women age 24 and under suffer from the highest rates of rape. **The Justice Department estimates that one in five women will experience rape or attempted rape** during their college years, and that **less than five percent of these rapes will be reported.** Income is also a factor: the poorer the household, the higher the rate of domestic violence — with women in the lowest income category experiencing more than six times the rate of nonfatal intimate partner violence as compared to women in the highest income category. When we consider race, we see that African-American women face higher rates of domestic violence than white women, and

## The CREEP Among Us * Anne Penn

American-Indian women are victimized at a rate more than double that of women of other races.

In honor of all the victims of murder solved and unsolved.

Amber Belken The GameStop Murder San Antonio Texas

I dedicate this page to Amber Marie Belken who was just 25 when her life was taken so viciously in a robbery/murder. Her mother Leigh says: "She was just getting ready to quit her job at GameStop and go back to school to study what her lifetime dream was. She wanted to be a veterinarian. She loved animals and dragged every stray she came across home. She was at the top of her game and ready to take on the world. She just stayed at GameStop a bit too long trying make a little more money before she quit. She was our only child and we miss her every second of every day. She was our life. Everything we did was based around her. She was very bright and very respectful of others. She was a one of a kind." Victim of murder. This case was solved and the criminal is behind bars forever. Hugs to Ambers parents who live with their loss every minute. You can see the pain in the eyes and in the expressions of victims of violent crimes and their families who are forever changed.

The thing is.... there are so many sexually based violent crimes against women that I could write volumes on just that alone. Even if I were to just list names of the women who are assaulted, raped, murdered, missing, exploited and trafficked one could still write volumes. Until we teach our children, ourselves, our spouses, our society a way to think differently about women, until we change the narrative we tell ourselves and others about equality and the value of human life, ALL life we will be stuck in the same patterns of abuse and violence against one another. It works both ways. There are women who perpetrate violence against men.

Change starts one person at a time. Even the words we use make a difference. Change begins today. One person at a time.

## Bibliography

The Suspected Golden State Killer Witnessed Two Men Rape His Sister. It May Have Fueled His Rampage. Stephanie K. Baer BuzzFeed News Reporter Last updated on May 14, 2018, at 4:35 p.m. ET

https://www.buzzfeednews.com/article/skbaer/the-suspected-golden-state-killer-witnessed-two-men-rape#.hxkX3BL4ZM

Sacramento Bee article 10-21-77 Warren Holloway & Thom Akeman

Newspaper articles are from archives posted onto the internet and are in public domain

https://en.wikipedia.org/wiki/Visalia_Ransacker

Sacramento Bee article May 18, 2018 by Sam Stanton Police are scouring

https://www.theguardian.com/us-news/2018/sep/15/are-american-serial-killers-a-dying-breed

Visalia Ransacker crimes, Wikipedia retrieved September 27, 2018 These reference materials are used as set forth under Section 107 (the Fair Use Doctrine) of the US Copyright Act and are used for educational and informational purposes only.

Images of the Visalia Ransacker crimes map partial timeline retrieved from Wikipedia September 2018

Images of Visalia Ransacker composites are from the internet images in public domain

https://www.sfgate.com/news/article/DNA-Links-70s-East-Area-Rapist-to-Serial-2935342.php

DNA graphic: Washington State graphics by Mark Nowlin The Seattle Times reporting by Sara Jean Green and the source is the Snohomish Sheriff's Office:

Images of murder victims are from images on the internet regarding the cases and are in public domain

Citrus Heights Sentenial article August 2018

http://www.latimes.com/local/obituaries/la-me-obit-marin-mazzie-20180913-story.html

2001 article DNA Links '70s 'East Area Rapist' to Serial Killings / Evidence suggests suspect moved to Southern California

**Erin Hallissy and Charlie Goodyear, Chronicle Staff Writers**
**Published 4:00 am PDT, Wednesday, April 4, 2001**
*Article by Joseph Serna and Benjamin Oresme's from the LA Times May 25, 2018*

http://www.endthebacklog.org/backlog/why-backlog-exists

http://www.visaliatimesdelta.com/story/opinion/2015/03/25/visalia-training-ground/70406130/

https://now.org/resource/violence-against-women-in-the-united-states-statistic/

Materials presented in this book that are photographs of victims were taken from the internet on various image sites. They are published for educational and informational purposes only in the interest of this book and I am using them as set forth under Section 107 (the Fair Use doctrine) of the U.S. Copyright Act of 1976.

News articles are published for educational and informational purposes only in the interest of this book and I am using them as set forth under Section 107 (the Fair Use doctrine) of the U.S. Copyright Act of 1976.

Leslie D'Ambrosia, Special Agent. "Florida Department Of Law Enforcement Miami Regional Operations Center in consultation and review by Detective Sergeant John Yarbrough, Los Angeles County Sheriff's Department Homicide Bureau." "http://www.ear-ons.com/nightstalkerprofile.pdf." *Ear-ons.com*. N.p., n.d. Web. 5 Oct. 2013.

Crompton, Larry. *Sudden Terror: The True Story of California's Most Infamous Sexual Predator, the East Area Rapist Aka the Original Night Stalker*. Bloomington IN: Authorhouse, 2010. Print.

Former Police Chief Nick Willick conversations on the telephone summer 2018

Photographs of all places in Auburn taken October 5, 2018 by Anne Penn copyright 2018

Shelby, Richard. *Hunting a Psychopath: The East Area Rapist: Original Night Stalker Investigation.* Bradenton, FL: BookLocker.com, 2015. Print. I am using a quote from this book as set forth under Section 107 (the Fair Use doctrine) of the U.S. Copyright Act of 1976.

"http://www.ear-ons.com/nightstalkerprofile.pdf." *Ear-ons.com.* N.p., n.d. Web. 7 Feb. 2016.

Photographs of ligatures and knots as well as footprint were retrieved from the internet and were listed under images in general

All of the information presented in this book is used for educational purposes and to inform the public.

Other resources on the cases also available on Amazon from the original detectives from Sacramento County and Contra Costa County:

**Case Files Sudden Terror by Larry Crompton 2010**

**Hunting a Psychopath by Richard Shelby 2014**

**Other books by Anne Penn:**

**Murder On His Mind Serial Killer** First Edition Published January 2017 used to get the word out. Blue Cover. This book does not contain as much personal connection but has investigative information about the crimes and the criminal. 364 pages

**Murder On His Mind The Original Night Stalker A Family Member Speaks** published in November

The CREEP Among Us * Anne Penn

2017 is the second edition which includes personal family connections as well as new information about Cold Cases, Rape and DNA. Right after the arrest of DeAngelo I added a few more chapters with a bit of what we knew about the man then. Cover is Black and Red with the blue eye. 510 pages currently

All books are available on Amazon and Barnes and Noble in paperback. Kindle versions are available on Amazon.

Anne Penn podcasts:

Dan Zupansky Blog Talk Radio July 2017

http://www.blogtalkradio.com/dan-zupansky1/2017/07/13/murder-on-his-mind-serial-killer-anne-penn

http://www.blogtalkradio.com/dan-zupansky1/2017/11/23/murder-on-his-mind-a-family-member-speaks-anne-penn

http://www.blogtalkradio.com/dan-zupansky1/2018/05/02/earons-golden-state-killer-unmasked-anne-penn

Alan Warren Seattle July 2017 KKNW Seattle

https://www.podomatic.com/podcasts/houseofmysteryradio/episodes/2017-07-08T13_00_03-07_00

Photographs from Auburn taken by Anne Penn AKA Laurie and are copyright protected October 2018

## Resources for Victims of Violent Crimes

Victims of Violent Crimes Resource Information

National Center for Victims of Crime

http://victimsofcrime.org/

http://victimsofcrime.org/help-for-crime-victims

Help for Crime Victims

The National Center for Victims of Crime has a number of resources available to assist victims of crime. Our National Help Line, VictimConnect, provides help for victims of any crime nationwide, and can be reached by phone at 1--855-4VICTIM (1-855-484-2846) or by online chat.

Find Law: http://criminal.findlaw.com/criminal-legal-help/crime-victim-resources.html

National Organization for Victim Assistance
http://www.trynova.org/

Sacramento County Website newsletter detailing the arrest of Joseph James DeAngelo. Retrieved October 2018

**** Note I may add a chapter of new information to this publication. If you purchase this book I will be happy to send via email any new chapters or information to you by request. All you have to do is email me at annepenn13@gmail.com, tell me of your purchase date of either kindle or paperback and I will email you any new chapter of information.

Made in the USA
Columbia, SC
14 November 2018